Veronica Heley has taught in Junior Church, run youth clubs, and been Events Organizer for the Association of Christian Writers. She gives talks and runs workshops for writers of all ages. She is author of over forty books, including Who, Me? Paul *and* The Easter Tree, *both published under the Barnabas imprint.*

Stories
of everyday
saints

Veronica Heley

40 stories with Bible links and related activities

Published by
The Bible Reading Fellowship
First Floor, Elsfield Hall
15–17 Elsfield Way, Oxford OX2 8FG

ISBN 1 84101 224 6
First published 2002
10 9 8 7 6 5 4 3 2 1 0

Acknowledgments
Unless otherwise stated, scripture quotations are taken from the *Contemporary English Version* © American Bible Society 1991, 1992, 1995. Used by permission/Anglicizations © British and Foreign Bible Society 1997.

Good News Bible published by The Bible Societies/HarperCollins Publishers Ltd, UK © American Bible Society 1966, 1971, 1976, 1992, used with permission.

Extract from *Is That It?* by Bob Geldof, published by Pan Macmillan, used by kind permission of the publishers.

A catalogue record for this book is available from the British Library

Printed and bound in Malta

Contents

Introduction

The forty men and women whose stories are told in this book may not have started out as perfect people, but they were used by God to do his work. Saints are people who listen to God and try to do what he wants.

The saints in this book fall into four categories:
- Bible saints from the New Testament, such as St Paul
- Historical and legendary saints, such as St George
- Worldwide saints, such as St Francis of Assisi
- More recent and contemporary saints, such as Mother Teresa

Some of the people have been formally named as saints by their church. In such cases, their name will appear with 'St' before it, as in St Patrick. Others have not been recognized publicly in this way, but are included in this book because God used them to carry out a particular task. These people are referred to simply by their ordinary names, such as Florence Nightingale.

The saints are given in this book in chronological order of their special days. So, for instance, in January we have Albert Schweitzer and in July we have St Christopher. This is so that, when appropriate, the story can tie in with a particular date.

There is an alphabetical index on pages 92–94 which also gives the era in which the saint lived, a key date, a brief note of his or her life, and a Bible reference.

Suggestions for activities

On each right-hand page there is a section for optional activities. Sometimes there is only one suggestion, suitable for all ages. Sometimes there are two activities, one intended for use by younger children, and one for older.

Occasionally three activities are suggested. Among these are suggestions for worksheets, crafts, drama, and creative writing.

Songs

I have given some suggestions for songs that tie in with the saint for the day, although you may have your own ideas.

Layout

There is a double page for each saint in this book, and on it you will find:
- A key date on which to remember the saint. This might be the date of birth or death, or the date of the formal recognition of that person as a saint
- A Bible reference, usually from the Contemporary English Version of the Bible (CEV)
- The story of the saint
- A prayer
- Suggestions for activities
- A symbol for the saint
- A suggested song or songs

In the middle of the book there is a photocopiable chart where all the saints' symbols are given. Each symbol can be coloured in as the children hear about the different saints.

St Kentigern (Mungo)

Key date: 13 January

Died 612.
Bishop of Strathclyde.
Started the legend that
gives Glasgow its arms of
ring and fish.

**When you give a feast, invite the poor,
the crippled, the lame, and the blind.**

LUKE 14:13

The ring and the fish

Do you have a pet name? Long ago there was a bishop who was loved so much that he, too, had a pet name. People called him Mungo, even though his real name was Kentigern. His cathedral in Glasgow is called St Mungo's, and his name is remembered today because St Mungo's charity in London still houses and looks after people sleeping rough on the streets.

Bishop Kentigern didn't have an easy life. He was a good man and always did his best to look after the people in his care, but then he fell foul of the politicians. One moment he was quietly doing his job in Glasgow, and the next he was sent into exile in Cumbria. Fortunately, he was able to return home after some years, and one particular story about him comes from the time when he got back.

The king of that part of Britain was very angry with his wife. She had given a precious ring of his to another man. You can imagine how well that went down with the king. He wrenched the ring back and, in a temper, he threw it far out to sea.

'Bring me back my ring within three days,' he said. 'Or else…!'

The queen was terribly upset. How on earth was she to recover the ring?

Bishop Kentigern heard all about it, and knew how sorry she was for having been so silly. He told her not to worry and… he produced the selfsame ring. One of his monks had caught a fine salmon and, on cutting it open to clean it, had discovered the missing ring inside.

That is how the great city of Glasgow came to have a ring and a fish on its coat of arms.

Prayer

Dear Father God, please look after the poor people who have nowhere to live.

Make a badge

You will need:
- ❂ Badges—these can be bought ready-made, or cut from card with a safety pin taped on to the back. Or you can use sticky labels
- ❂ Pencils or coloured pens or crayons to decorate the badges with

Draw a symbol to fit into your badge, using the things you like best, or the symbol you would choose, to show people what you are like. Colour it in.

Thinking about symbols

The city of Glasgow has a ring and fish as its emblem or badge, to remind everyone about St Mungo. Think what symbol or symbols you would choose, to show people what you are like. If you are a musician, it might be a musical note or a recorder; a mathematician might use a geometrical shape. Someone who is fond of reading might like a book; someone who likes flowers might like a plant; and a footballer could have a ball going into the net!

Then make your own badge.

Symbol

Suggested song

Stand up, stand up for Jesus (JP226)

Albert Schweitzer

Key date: 14 January

1875–1965.
Nobel Prize winner,
musician, philosopher,
doctor. Founded and
worked in a hospital in
French Equatorial Africa.

Schweitzer said, 'No way of life makes more sense than the way taught by Jesus.'

'I am the way, the truth, and the life!'

JOHN 14:6

The man with four hats

Let's count how many careers Albert Schweitzer had. As a boy, he was so clever at music that everyone thought he would make it his career. He wrote a study of the musician, Bach, and everyone said, 'Well, that proves it. Albert Schweitzer's going to be a great musician.' (That's one!)

He went to university to study the life of Jesus and wrote a brilliant book about that, too. Now he had a choice of careers, music or preaching. (That's two!) But then another career turned up, because he happened to read about the needs of the poorest, sickest people in Africa. He decided to throw up his comfortable life in Europe and study all over again, this time to become…

a doctor. Six years later he was ready. He raised money by giving organ recitals and talks, and went out to the Congo to help the people there. (That makes three!)

His hospital was a very basic building, but as soon as he moved in, sick people started to arrive. He worked from dawn to dusk, helping them.

When the Second World War came, some local officials were suspicious of Schweitzer because he'd been born in a town in Europe which had once been part of Germany. He had to stop working as a doctor and was sent to France until the war ended and he could once more return to his hospital.

While he was waiting for the war to end, he started on his fourth career and wrote another famous book. This time his subject was the ideas people have about the way we live. This book won the highest award there is, called the Nobel Prize. What a man! Four careers in one lifetime! That takes a bit of doing, doesn't it?

Prayer

Our Father, help me to work hard and make the most of the gifts you have given me.

 **Suggested activities**

If the cap fits…

Can you see what Albert Schweitzer would use, or how he would look, in each of his different careers? Draw lines to link the picture to the right career.

Musician   Minister   Author   Doctor

First Aid

How much First Aid do you know? For example, what would you do if a friend had a fall in the playground? Or cut a finger badly? What would you do if you accidentally burned yourself at home?

Symbol

Where did he work? FOR OLDER CHILDREN

Use an atlas to find whereabouts Albert Schweitzer worked in Africa. What is that part of Africa called nowadays?

Suggested songs

Bind us together, Lord (JP17; C22)
Jesus' hands were kind hands (JP134; K194)

Reproduced with permission from *Stories of Everyday Saints* published by BRF 2002 (1 84101 224 6)

St Caedmon

Shout praises to the Lord, everyone on this earth. Be joyful and sing as you come in to worship the Lord!

PSALM 100:1–2

The song writer

Caedmon couldn't sing to save his life. It had bothered him a lot when he was younger, but now that he was getting on in years, he accepted it. He was thankful that, even though he could neither read nor write, he still had a good job. He looked after the cattle in a big monastery in the north of England. The cows didn't care that he couldn't sing and he always left the great hall after supper before it was his turn to entertain the guests.

One evening he fell asleep in his cowshed and had a strange dream. A man called him by name and said, 'Caedmon, sing me a song.'

'I don't know how,' said Caedmon.

'You can sing to me. Sing about the Creation.'

In his dream Caedmon began to sing in praise of God, in words he had never heard before and in perfect tune! When he woke up, he could remember exactly what he'd sung and found himself adding more words to the tune. Even to his own ears, his voice sounded different. He went to the estate manager and told him what had happened. Then he was called to see the head of the monastery, the great Abbess Hilda.

The abbess was amazed that this totally uneducated man could sing about God—even if he could only do it in his rough-and-ready English dialect instead of in the proper Latin. She put Caedmon through all sorts of tests, telling him stories from the Bible and asking him to make up songs about them, which Caedmon now found that he could do.

Soon people were singing Caedmon's songs far and wide, and this elderly man—who hadn't been able to sing before—became the pop star of his day.

Prayer

Dear Lord, please help me to use wisely whatever gifts you choose to give me

 **Suggested activities**

Have a good sing!

Sing Hallelu. Divide the group into two. Appoint a cheerleader for each section and see which one can sing louder!

One side sings:	The other side sings:
Hallelu, hallelu, hallelu, halleluia	
	We'll praise the Lord!
Hallelu, hallelu, hallelu, halleluia	
	We'll praise the Lord!
	We'll praise the Lord!
Halleluia	
	We'll praise the Lord!
Halleluia	
	We'll praise the Lord!
Halleluia	

(Both sides:) WE'LL PRAISE THE LORD!

Symbol

Repeat, with both sides seated to start with. They then stand to sing their own part, and sit after it. This takes some concentration and leads to lots of mistakes, especially when taken quickly.

Alternatively, divide the children into four groups and sing the song as a round, with each group in turn standing for 'We'll praise the Lord!' (Don't do this if the walls are thin and you are likely to disturb other classes.)

Make up a poem

Make up a poem in praise of God's world. Make up some words of praise to God, using the tune of a well-known song.

Suggested songs

Hallelu (JP67; C76)
Jesus bids us shine (JP128)
Morning has broken (JP166; C153)

Reproduced with permission from *Stories of Everyday Saints* published by BRF 2002 (1 84101 224 6)

Martin Luther

Key date: 18 February

1483–1546.
Leader of Reformation and
inspiration for rise of
Protestantism.

You cannot make God accept you because
of something you do. God accepts sinners
only because they have faith in him.

ROMANS 4:5

The hammer that split the Church

Do you keep quiet when you see something wrong, or
do you do something about it?

Martin Luther was Professor of Theology at a German
university. He heard people muttering that the Church
was in a bad way. People could do something terribly
wrong and buy their way out of trouble by giving money
to the Church. The priests didn't care how badly they
behaved, because the people at the top were no better!
Martin decided to do something about it.

Now, when somebody wanted to discuss a problem at
the university, they nailed a notice about it to the church
door. One day, Martin marched out with a hammer and
nailed a notice to the church door. Only this time it
wasn't about university affairs. This time he listed all the
things that he saw were wrong in the Church.

Half the people said, 'How dare he?' and the other
half said, 'Well, he's got something there!'

People began to take sides. Before you knew it, the
Pope was involved and Martin was had up in court, in
fear of his life! And then—he vanished! Months later, his
followers discovered that Martin had been kidnapped
by one of his friends and swept off to a remote castle, to
get him out of harm's way.

In the castle, he worked out that you didn't become
a Christian through doing good but because you
believed in and loved Jesus Christ.

War broke out between Martin's supporters—who
became known as Protestants—and those who upheld
the Pope's authority. The Catholic Church eventually
reformed itself, but by that time the Protestants had
broken away and the split in the Church has lasted from
that day to this. And it all started with a hammer and a nail.

Prayer

Dear Lord Jesus, help me to see when something goes
wrong with a friend, and then help me to see what I
can do to help.

Suggested activities

Draw and paint a castle

FOR YOUNGER CHILDREN

Draw a fairytale castle on a mountain top, with lots of turrets. This is to be Martin Luther's home, to keep him safe from his enemies.

Write a petition

FOR OLDER CHILDREN

Divide into two groups. Both groups have to prepare a petition to the head teacher. One group will focus on what improvements they would like to see made to the school buildings, to the playground, the library, or school lunches. The other group will make a list of rules that they would like to see about pupils' conduct at school. These must be positive suggestions, not negative.

Symbol

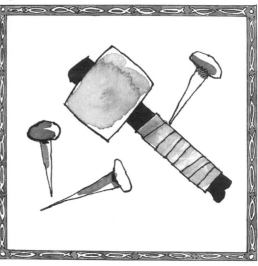

Suggested songs

Father, hear the prayer we offer (JP41)
Church is not a building (K27)

Reproduced with permission from *Stories of Everyday Saints* published by BRF 2002 (1 84101 224 6)

Gladys Aylward

**Key date:
24 February**

1902–1970.
Known as the
'Small Woman'.
Parlourmaid
who rescued
one hundred
Chinese children
during the war
against Japan.

Jesus led many of God's children to be
saved and to share in his glory.

HEBREWS 2:10

Jesus said, 'Let the children come to me!'

MARK 10:14

The small woman

You can be very small and not much good at reading or writing, but God can still use you. Gladys' father was a postman. She herself worked in a shop, as a children's nanny, and as a parlourmaid. She learned about the problems in China through church, and she realized that that was where she wanted to be. But how? She earned so little and couldn't speak the language. It all seemed quite impossible.

Then Gladys heard that a Mrs Jeannie Lawson, a widow, needed someone to help her in her work in north China. But there was no money for the fare.

Gladys sat on her bed and counted out the few pence she had saved. She said, 'Dear God, here's me, here's my Bible, here's my money! Use us!' Jesus was very real to her, and she consulted him at every turn.

Gladys was 30 before she had scraped together enough money for the journey. She set off from Liverpool Street Station and travelled halfway round the world to find Mrs Lawson.

In that part of China, there were no proper roads. Everything was carried on the backs of mules, so the two women opened an inn for the muleteers—a cross between a roadside caff for lorry drivers and a cheap motel. Gladys learned Chinese by ear, and became well known as a vivid teller of stories about Jesus.

In the Second World War, China was invaded by Japan. Many terrified children drifted around the countryside, without anyone to look after them. Gladys gathered together one hundred children and led them across the Yellow River to safety. A book called *The Small Woman* was written about this amazing adventure, and later it was turned into a famous film called *The Inn of the Sixth Happiness*.

Prayer

Dear Lord Jesus, help me to carry out the work you have planned for me to do, even when everything seems to be against me.

Suggested activities

Games to play

Play 'Follow my leader'. Whatever the leader does, you must copy. For example, hop, run on the spot, pat the top of your head, and finally sit cross-legged on the ground.

Play 'Granny's Footsteps'. Sneak up on the soldier on guard, without him seeing you. If he turns round and does see you, you have to go back to the beginning and start again.

The old China and the new

FOR OLDER CHILDREN

Explain the old custom of binding the feet of well-to-do Chinese girls, so that they could hardly walk. If possible, show a pair of tiny Chinese slippers. Gladys Aylward was made the local Inspector of Feet to make sure girls' feet were no longer bound in that cruel way, since soon after she arrived a law was passed forbidding it. The boys and men used to have the front of their heads shaved, and their back hair tied in a pigtail as a sign of submission to the Emperor of China.

Colour in two pictures. One shows a Chinese boy and girl as they used to be dressed. The other picture shows a modern-day Chinese boy and girl.

Symbol

Suggested song

He's got the whole world (JP78; C82)

Reproduced with permission from *Stories of Everyday Saints* published by BRF 2002 (1 84101 224 6)

St David

Key date: 1 March

Died 601.
Patron saint of Wales.
Vegetarian who believed
in hard work and
straight talking.

Love should always make us tell the truth.
Then we will grow in every way and be
more like Christ.

EPHESIANS 4:15

The vegetarian

Hands up anyone who doesn't eat meat!

This is a story about a saint who didn't eat meat. David was born and bred in Wales, and wanted nothing more than to serve God. He learned as much as he could at school and then went to study under a wise man on an island for another ten years. Think of it as going to university and staying there for ten years.

When David became a monk, he set out to live a pure, clean life. He wanted to be strong in mind and body so that he could help others. He decided to set himself a routine that would build up his muscles—in body as well as in spirit. He would work hard, study hard, and eat only bread and vegetables. Moreover, while everyone else drank wine or beer as a matter of course, he would only drink water. He founded ten monasteries where the monks all lived in the same way, working hard and studying hard.

David was kind to everyone who needed help, but if they said something silly, he made a point of putting them right. At that time some people were going around talking a lot of nonsense about God. Eventually, a big meeting was called to discuss the matter. David spoke so much good sense and explained the truth about God's ways so clearly that he was made head of the church in Wales.

The story goes that the Welsh adopted the leek as their badge because it was one of David's favourite vegetables. When they went to war, Welshmen pinned a leek to their jackets to show that they were Welsh. Later on, the daffodil became popular instead. Like many other Welshmen, David is said to have had a beautiful voice.

Prayer

Dear Lord Jesus, show me how to prepare myself to serve you.

Suggested activities

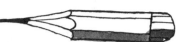

Dot to dot `FOR YOUNGER CHILDREN`

Join the dots to find one of David's symbols.

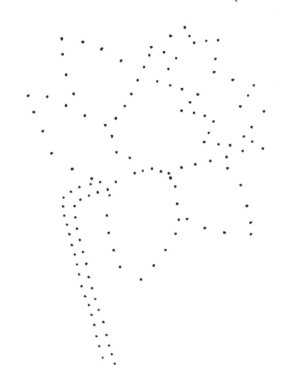

Symbol

Diet `FOR OLDER CHILDREN`

Have a discussion about vegetarianism—how to get a balanced diet without meat. Talk about what happens if you don't get the balance right.

FRUIT & VEG   CEREALS   CRUNCH   FLAKES   OATS   BREKIE

Reproduced with permission from *Stories of Everyday Saints* published by BRF 2002 (1 84101 224 6)

St Frances of Rome

**Key date:
9 March**

Patron saint of
motorists. Wife and
mother, in riches
and in poverty she
tended the sick,
especially those
with the plague.
She could see her
guardian angel.

**God will command his angels to protect you
wherever you go.**

PSALM 91:11

**You hold my right hand. Your advice has
been my guide.**

PSALM 73:23–24

The angel in the car

Did you know there was a special saint for motorists?
Frances was born into a wealthy Roman family many
years ago, long before cars were invented. She was
married at the age of 13 and had six children, whom she
loved very much. But, not content with managing her
household, she began looking after poor people,
especially those in hospital.

Have you ever heard of the plague? It was a terrible
disease which could kill a whole family in hours. The
doctors and nurses were often the first to die, because
they caught it from their patients. Frances could have
fled the city as so many other rich people did. But no,
she stayed to nurse the sick.

Worse was to come. Rome was captured by armed
forces and the family house and estates were targeted.
Somehow, Frances managed to keep everyone going
while continuing her work with the poor.

For Frances had a secret weapon. She loved God so
much that she had been allowed to see her guardian
angel. Do you know about guardian angels? We've all
got them. They do their best to keep us out of trouble,
even though we can't usually see them.

Frances' angel advised her what to do all the time
and kept her safe, even when people all around her
were dying of the plague. Several other women helped
her in looking after the sick, and they decided to wear a
simple uniform of black gown and white hood. Her
house still exists in Rome and people can go to visit it.
But even if we can't go to Rome to see her house or the
church which was named after her, we can remember
her—and our guardian angels—when we cross a busy
road, or get into a car.

Prayer

Dear Lord, help me to listen to my guardian angel at all
times.

Suggested activities

Safety first

Remind the children of road safety. Remember that angels obey the rules of the road! Some people say that if you run a red light, you leave your angel behind and it may take a little while before they catch up with you again!

Ring o' roses

Teach the children the nursery rhyme 'Ring o' roses' and tell them how it was inspired by the plague. One sign of the disease was a raised red ring on your skin—the roses of the song. People carried sweet-smelling herbs in a posy, which they hoped would ward off the infection. A sneeze was one of the first signs that you had caught the disease, and then you dropped down—dead!

Symbol

FOR OLDER CHILDREN

Road code

Draw a map showing the roads around the school or in the centre of town, where pedestrian crossings and traffic intersections may be hazardous. Talk about how to cross these roads safely.

Invite a lollipop lady or man—who is like a guardian angel on the road—to visit the classroom to talk about their work.

Suggested songs

Anytime, anywhere, I can talk to God (C18)
Don't you worry about tomorrow (K43)

George Muller

**When you welcome even a child because
of me, you welcome me.**

MARK 9:37

Father to thousands
of children

150 years ago, children without parents lived on the streets, or were herded into workhouses where they often died young. God used a young German to do something about it. George Muller was a minister in Bristol. Unlike other preachers, he refused to accept a salary but depended upon God for everything he needed.

George couldn't bear to see the children on the streets, so he rented a house where orphaned children could be fed, clothed, taught a trade, and equipped to earn their own living. Soon there were two houses, and then three. Still the numbers of children on the waiting list grew. George set about buying land and building new houses specially for his children.

He never asked anybody except God for money. He prayed: money and gifts arrived. One day the children were standing at their tables before breakfast. There were empty plates on the tables, nothing in the larder, and no money to buy food. Muller lifted up his hands and prayed, 'Father, we thank you for what you are going to give us to eat.'

A knock was heard at the door and there stood the baker. 'I couldn't sleep last night. I felt you didn't have bread for breakfast, and the Lord wanted me to send you some. So I got up at two o'clock and baked some fresh bread for you.'

Muller thanked the baker and praised God for his care. There was a second knock at the door. This time it was the milkman. His cart had broken down outside the orphanage, and he wanted to give the children his cans of fresh milk, so that he could empty his wagon and repair it.

Thousands of children called George Muller their father. Prayer—in faith—works.

Prayer

Loving Father, you know our needs even better than we do. In the name of Jesus, we ask for your love in our lives.

 # Suggested activity

Help one another

There are many charities supporting children. Talk about some of these, and ask the children what charities they know about, and what each one does. Help the children to organize a fund-raising event for the one that appeals to them most.

Symbol

The Field Lane Homeless Families unit in King's Cross is a day centre which, among other activities, arranges parties at Christmas for all on their books. Every year they set out to provide presents for up to 200 children who would otherwise have nothing. Funds and gifts arrive out of the blue. One year an old lady knitted seventeen outfits for Barbie dolls, but couldn't find anyone who wanted them because she had no dolls to fit them. Field Lane were given a bag full of naked Barbie dolls, and seventeen children were made happy with unexpected presents.

Field Lane's address is Field Lane Foundation, 16 Vine Hill, London EC1R 5EA.

(Regd charity No 207493)

Suggested songs

When I needed a neighbour (JP275; C229)
Streets of grey (St S10)

Reproduced with permission from *Stories of Everyday Saints* published by BRF 2002 (1 84101 224 6)

St Patrick

Key date: 17 March

5th century.
A slave in Ireland for six years. Returning to England, he was made a bishop and sent back to Ireland, where he fought paganism.

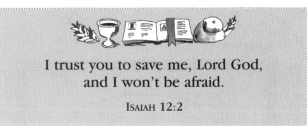

I trust you to save me, Lord God, and I won't be afraid.

ISAIAH 12:2

The slave

Do you know what a slave is? It's someone who has to work without any pay and is often badly treated. Pirates don't raid London or Birmingham nowadays, do they? But in the old days, even living in the West Midlands didn't make you safe. One moment young Patrick was the happy-go-lucky son of a town councillor living far inland, and the next he was carried off by Irish raiders and sold as a slave. For six long years he looked after his master's cattle in Ireland. He struggled through to become a Christian, placing his life completely in God's hands.

One night he had a wonderful dream: soon he would be on his way home. After many hair-raising adventures, he found a ship to take him back to England. His family found him much changed. Can you imagine what a marvellous party they had to celebrate?

Patrick now wanted to spend his life in the service of God. He'd missed a lot of schooling, but he did get some training and became a priest. Where do you think he was sent when he was appointed a bishop? Back to Ireland!

There was a lot to be done. The Irish were worshipping the sun and strange idols. Patrick knew that some people would look down on him because he hadn't been to college, but he trusted God to tell him what to say, and he never forgot that God had rescued him from a life of slavery.

The best story about Patrick is that he is supposed to have cleared Ireland of snakes, and it's true that to this day there are no poisonous snakes in that beautiful green land. It's also said that he was the first one to explain the Trinity with the aid of the three-lobed shamrock leaf.

Prayer

Dear Lord, in bad times and in good, help me to trust you completely.

Suggested activities

Make your own snake!

You will need:
- ❂ Green plasticine
- ❂ A pencil or ballpoint pen
- ❂ Red felt or paper
- ❂ Scissors

Make a wiggly snake by rolling a lump of green plasticine backwards and forwards under the palm of your hand. The head should be fattest, and the body should taper away to the tail. Cut a forked tongue out of red felt or paper. Make a 'mouth' in the head of the snake with your fingertip, insert the blunt end of the tongue, and squash the head down on the tongue. Push the point of the ballpoint pen or pencil into either side of the head to make two eye sockets.

Sew a snake!

You will need:
- ❂ A rectangle of green felt
- ❂ Tissue or other soft paper
- ❂ A small piece of red felt
- ❂ A needle
- ❂ Buttons
- ❂ Thread
- ❂ Scissors
- ❂ Fabric glue

Sew the long sides of the rectangle of green felt together to make a tube. Insert a triangle of red felt (broad side into the 'head') and sew across that end, including the 'tongue' in the stitching. Stuff the body with soft paper, and sew up the tail end. Sew, or stick, two buttons, one on either side of the head, to make the eyes.

Symbol

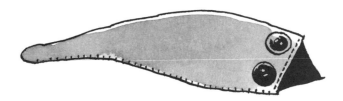

'Three in one'

Discuss what other symbols, apart from the shamrock leaf, represent the three-in-one of God. For example: water can be present as liquid, steam or ice; an egg contains the shell, white and yolk.

Suggested songs

Father, lead me day by day (JP43)
It is March 17th (BBP50)

Reproduced with permission from *Stories of Everyday Saints* published by BRF 2002 (1 84101 224 6)

St Joseph of Arimathea

Key date: 17 March

1st century.
He took Jesus' body and
put it in his own tomb. His
staff became the Holy
Thorn of Glastonbury.

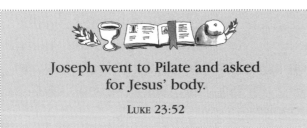

**Joseph went to Pilate and asked
for Jesus' body.**

LUKE 23:52

The Thorn of Glastonbury

Jesus had been sentenced to death by the High Council of the Jews, who hated him. Not everyone agreed with the verdict. A man called Joseph—who had always tried to do good—objected strongly. He knew Jesus personally, and he knew that Jesus was innocent.

But Jesus was to die, and Joseph could do nothing to prevent it. He could only watch and grieve. After it was all over and Jesus was pronounced dead, Joseph realized that there *was* something he could do. He was a rich man and well known in the city. So he went to see the Roman governor, Pontius Pilate, and said, 'Will you let me have Jesus' body?'

Pilate agreed and gave Joseph an order to the soldiers to that effect. Joseph took Jesus' body down from the cross. He wrapped it in a long linen cloth and laid it in a new cave-like tomb in the rock, one that he had had prepared for himself. Night was approaching and soon it would be the day of rest, when no work could be carried out. So Joseph secured the tomb by rolling a great stone across its mouth.

The Bible tells us that three days later, Jesus' friends found the tomb empty. After Jesus rose from the dead, the story goes that Joseph left Jerusalem and travelled widely, spreading the good news wherever he went. His route was up through France and into England, where he and his followers were given what was then an island rising out of the marshes. There Joseph planted his staff, and it grew into the Holy Thorn tree which flowers at Christmas time. The marshes around that island were eventually drained and the island is now a hill which can be seen for miles.

Today people still travel to Glastonbury to see the descendant of Joseph's thorn tree.

Prayer

Dear Lord God, when you need something done, help me to see what it is and to do the right thing.

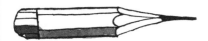 

Suggested activities

Make a flowering staff

You will need:
- ✪ A green or brown straw
- ✪ Tissue paper: green and pink and white
- ✪ Glue
- ✪ Scissors

Make rosettes from 6cm squares of tissue paper in different colours. Glue them to the top of the straw, to represent Joseph's Flowering Thorn.

Symbol

Make a flowering staff

You will need:
- ✪ Two brown or green straws, one thicker, one thinner. The thinner one should go inside the thicker one
- ✪ Narrow, shiny Christmas wrapping tape in pink and green, the type that you can curl
- ✪ Sticky tape
- ✪ Scissors

Suggested songs

Low in the grave (JP159)
Now the green blade (JP174)

Cut 5 cm off the bottom of the larger straw. Cut two 6cm lengths of pink tape, and two of the green (or three of green, and one of pink). Squeeze the end of the bunch and insert into one end of the narrower straw. Bind with sticky tape; try to use the sticky tape only once round.

Wind the narrow straw and tassel down into the tube, 'flower' end last, till the tassel is completely hidden. Then push the stick up from the bottom so that the tassel 'flowers' out of the top end. Curl the green and pink tape with the back of the scissors.

Reproduced with permission from *Stories of Everyday Saints* published by BRF 2002 (1 84101 224 6)

St Cuthbert

**Key date:
20 March**

c.634–687.
The hermit
bishop who
loved the
solitude of
the island of
Inner Farne.
Very popular
in the north
of England.

'Love the Lord your God with all your heart,
soul, strength, and mind… Love your
neighbours as much as you love yourself.'

LUKE 10:27

The man who liked to be quiet

Have you ever wanted to be quiet when your friends
wanted you to go and play with them? Cuthbert was like
that. More than anything else in the world, he wanted to
live alone to praise God. But his friends were always
dragging him back to look after them.

You see, Cuthbert was good at looking after people.
When he was put in charge of Melrose Abbey, he turned
out to be the sort of man to whom everyone goes in
times of trouble. The plague came and many local
people put their faith in devilish spells—until Cuthbert
went travelling around, helping them to hold on to the
love of God, and showing them how to love their
neighbours. After some years, he was transferred to

Lindisfarne and then he was able to escape to his
beloved Inner Farne island and be quiet for a change.

His friends said, 'You can't possibly live on that rocky
little island! Nothing will grow there and there's not
even any water to drink.' Cuthbert told them to dig a
well in the floor of his little stone house—and the next
day it had filled with water. He planted barley and, even
though it was far too late in the season, a good crop
quickly sprang up.

Cuthbert's friends thought it would be a good idea
to make him a bishop. Cuthbert didn't want to leave his
peaceful island, but he couldn't refuse. He went back to
Lindisfarne as bishop, but in the end he managed to die
in the place he had loved so much, on that rocky little
island in the sea. Today the Farne Islands are a bird
sanctuary run by the National Trust. Cuthbert would
have liked that, wouldn't he?

Prayer

Dear Lord Jesus, help me to be quiet sometimes, so
that I can listen to what you are telling me.

Suggested activities

Colour for Cuthbert

Colour in the drawing of St Cuthbert with some of his much-loved wildlife on Lindisfarne.

Colour and name Cuthbert's favourites

Match the list of names to the sea life in the drawings.

Seaweed

Puffin

Starfish

Gull

Grey seal

Seagrass

Eider duck

Seashells

Symbol

Suggested songs

Father, we adore you (JP44)
First the seed and then the rain (BBP51)

Reproduced with permission from *Stories of Everyday Saints* published by BRF 2002 (1 84101 224 6)

Martin Luther King

Key date: 4 April
(Also a national holiday
in the USA: third
Monday in January)

Born 1929,
assassinated 4 April,
1968. Leader of the
US black freedom
movement. Nobel
Peace Prize winner.

On us who live in the dark shadow of
death this light will shine to guide us into
a life of peace.

LUKE 1:79

'I have a dream'

Martin was both black and clever. He was a Baptist minister, like his father and grandfather. He could see that although black people in America weren't slaves any more, they still didn't have the same rights as white people. They couldn't sit in a bus if a white person needed a seat. They couldn't be served in the same eating-places, or use the parks on equal terms. Above all, they weren't equal before the law.

The people were getting very angry and rebelling against these conditions. Martin saw that this could only lead to bloodshed. He asked God for guidance and he prayed about it. In the end he decided to preach the cause of non-violent protest.

'I have a dream,' he said, 'that all men some day will be brothers.'

Black people listened and followed him in great demonstrations which never turned to violence. The ideas behind his speeches caught the imagination of white people and before long they acknowledged that he was right in what he said. All people are born equal and should have the same rights under the law. The American government voted to end some of the worst abuses from which the ethnic minorities had been suffering.

Martin didn't only work for black people. He wanted to help poor people of all races and he wanted to see an end to wars.

In 1964, Martin Luther King was voted the Nobel Peace Prize because he had inspired the black freedom movement with such wisdom and humanity that it became an unstoppable crusade. Unfortunately, not everyone shared his beliefs and he was shot and killed when he was only 39 years old. There is a national holiday for him in America on the third Monday in January.

Prayer

Dear Father God, guide me always to speak with your words, to bring peace where there is war, and love where there is hate.

Suggested activities

Children playing together

Draw a picture of your own, or colour in this picture, which shows all races and colours of children playing happily together.

A poem or story about peace

Write a poem or a story about someone who makes peace between people who are quarrelling.

Symbol

Suggested songs

Brothers and sisters (JP21; K17)
The prophet had a vision (St S15)
A dream to share (St S63)

Reproduced with permission from *Stories of Everyday Saints* published by BRF 2002 (1 84101 224 6)

St Bernadette

Key date: 16 April

Visionary of Lourdes.
The simple peasant girl
whose visions of the Virgin
Mary began the pilgrimages
to Lourdes.

Mary said, 'I am the Lord's servant… With
all my heart I praise the Lord, and I am glad
because of God my Saviour.'

LUKE 1:38, 46–47

The miller's daughter

Marie-Bernarde didn't have an easy life. She was small
for her age and the eldest of the miller's nine children.
What's more, she suffered from asthma. When she was
14, an extraordinary thing happened. She saw Mary, the
mother of Jesus—Our Lady—on a rock face not far from
her home. The Lady told Marie-Bernarde to drink from
a spring that began to gush out of the dry rock.

Over the next six months, Marie-Bernarde saw the
Lady many more times. The Lady told her that she
wanted a church built on that spot. She wanted
everyone to be sorry for all the bad things they had
done, and turn to praising God. That was just fine by
Marie-Bernarde.

But her parents didn't think it was fine. Nor did the
local ministers of the church. Nor did the mayor. They
said, 'Why should Our Lady appear to a poor little
creature like Marie-Bernarde when there are so many
more important people she could have spoken to?'

Word got around that the water from the new spring
at the rock face could heal you. Marie-Bernarde was
questioned again, this time by ministers and state
officials. She knew what she'd seen and heard, and she
couldn't be shaken in her story. Then began the great
pilgrimages to the rock face. Everyone wanted to see
Marie-Bernarde. They gave her no peace till she went as
a boarder to a school nearby and eventually became a
nun. She had nothing to do with the great church that
was eventually built at the rock face, or with the tours
which have taken so many sick people to Lourdes every
year since. She was a straightforward person who
passed on the message she'd been given. Today we call
her Saint Bernadette of Lourdes.

Prayer

Dear Lord Jesus, help me to be truthful in all things.

Suggested activity

Taste and tell!

What do you think the spring water at Lourdes tastes like?

Have a blind tasting session with different drinks. Have some blindfolds ready and approximately eight containers filled with different liquids. Label the containers A–H (depending on how many you have). Provide lots of small taster cups. See how many you can identify without looking.

Suggested drinks: tomato juice, orange squash, real orange juice, cold tea, cold coffee, milk, Coca-Cola, fizzy or tonic water.

Symbol

Suggested song

Have you heard the raindrops? (JP71; K99; C78)

St George

We are not fighting against humans. We are fighting against… rulers of darkness… So put on all the armour that God gives.

EPHESIANS 6:12–13

St George for England

Once upon a time a fire-breathing dragon arrived in a far country. The dragon was covered with green scales and had a long tail which could knock a man off his feet.

The king sent some foot soldiers to confront the evil creature. They were all scattered and killed. Then the kingdom's bravest knights went out to do battle with the dragon. None returned alive.

A terrible silence fell on the land. The king announced that he required two sheep a day to keep the dragon quiet. After a while, there were no more sheep left. It was decided that a young girl would be provided instead. To make matters fair, the maiden would be chosen by lot. One day it was the turn of the king's only daughter.

The princess wept as she was led out to the dragon's lair, but there was nothing anyone could do to save her. Or was there?

Galloping across the plain on a white horse came a knight in shining armour. But what could he do when so many other men had tried and failed? Well, this was St George, and he was different. He felt fear—of course he did—but he trusted in God and he didn't let his fear prevent him from tackling the great beast. As the dragon reared up, the knight spurred his horse on faster, ever faster, levelling his sharp lance at the one place between the beast's front leg and breast which was not covered with thick scales. The point of the lance drove home. The dragon screamed with pain and fury and the lance broke off. The dragon sent a blast of fire in the direction of the knight… but St George circled behind the beast and cut off its head with his trusty sword.

Prayer

Dear Father God, help me to be brave enough to tackle evil—with your help.

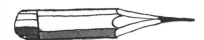 

Suggested activity

Stage a play!

Stage a play with cardboard lance, sword and shield. The story can be read by some of the children, while others act out the drama.

You will need:
- ✪ Readers
- ✪ King and queen
- ✪ St George
- ✪ Dragon
- ✪ Citizens to weep and wail
- ✪ Farmers (to say that there are no more sheep)
- ✪ Ordinary soldiers
- ✪ Brave knights
- ✪ Princess

Suggested songs

Be bold, be strong (JP14)
April 23rd is here again (BBP50)
When a knight won his spurs (K371)

Symbol

NB: The original saint was a soldier martyred about AD303 in Palestine. He became England's patron saint during the Crusades, and was adopted by many other countries as well. The dragon-slaying legend arose in the 12th century. The dragon represents evil and the maiden represents a place menaced by evil.

St Mark

**Key date:
25 April**

Died c.74.
Author of the
Gospel that bears
his name. Cousin
of Barnabas,
companion of
Paul and Peter.
Patron of Venice.

Mark, who is like a son to me, sends his
greetings too.

1 PETER 5:13

This is the good news about Jesus Christ,
the Son of God.

MARK 1:1

The eye-witness

Do you know a child who always manages to be around
when something important is going on—even when
they're not supposed to be there?

Mark was too young to be one of the twelve special
friends of Jesus, but when they were in Jerusalem, Jesus
and his friends often stayed at the house that belonged
to Mark's mother. It was there that Jesus and his friends
ate their Last Supper together. Afterwards, they went
out to the garden on the Mount of Olives—and Mark
secretly followed them. When Jesus was arrested, all his
friends—including Mark—ran away. Mark only just
escaped arrest by the soldiers, too.

Mark had a cousin called Barnabas, who was one of
the first to leave Jerusalem to spread the good news
about Jesus. Barnabas invited Mark to go travelling
along with him and St Paul. Perhaps Mark was a little too
young to appreciate someone as single-minded as Paul.
Whatever the reason, within months Mark left and went
back home to Jerusalem. Paul was furious. Later, when
Barnabas planned to go travelling again with Paul, he
said, 'Let's give young Mark a second chance.' Paul
wouldn't hear of it, and the two men fell out. So
Barnabas took Mark with him while Paul went off in
another direction.

As he grew older and wiser, Mark made it up with
Paul. Mark even travelled to Rome to look after Paul
when he was imprisoned there. Mark grew to be such a
loving person that both Paul and St Peter—Jesus' right-
hand man—talked about him as their 'son'. It was Peter
who gave Mark what information he didn't already have
about Jesus' life, and Mark's Gospel was the first written
report on Jesus' miracles, his death and his resurrection.

Prayer

Dear Father God, please help me to be a loving and
helpful friend, especially to those who are much older
than myself.

Suggested activity

Make a model lion for Mark

St Mark's symbol is a winged lion.

You will need:
- ❂ A photocopy of the model
- ❂ Medium weight card
- ❂ Crayons or paints
- ❂ Scissors
- ❂ Glue

Using the photocopied model as a template, cut out the lion with its wings and the strap in medium-weight card. Colour all parts. Carefully cut the slots in the lion. Crease the lion along its backbone, and the strap along the dotted lines as shown. Insert the wings into the 'shoulders' of the lion and glue into place. Fold the lion in half. Glue the strap along the creased edges. Place the strap inside the lion and glue firmly in place. Glue along inside of the lion's nose and one tail piece and press the model together at these points to form one face and one tail.

Symbol

Suggested songs

Here is the news (S89)
Go, tell it on the mountain (JP65; C250)

Reproduced with permission from *Stories of Everyday Saints* published by BRF 2002 (1 84101 224 6)

Lord Shaftesbury

Key date: born 28 April

1801–1885.
Although nobly born, he fought
for the poor—especially for the
chimney-sweep children.

'A man's religion… should enter every sphere of his life.' (Shaftesbury)

God is Spirit, and those who worship God must be led by the Spirit to worship him according to the truth.

JOHN 4:24

The chimney sweep's friend

A hundred years ago, not many of you would have been lucky enough to go to school. You would have been sent out to work instead. Some of you would have worked twelve hours a day in the coal-mines, or in noisy factories. Some might have had a job on a farm, but others would have been working as chimney sweeps.

Which would have been worse—working down a mine or being given a brush and pushed up a hot chimney? Some of the chimneys were old and had kinks in them, so even the longest brushes couldn't get through. But small boys could get round the corners, couldn't they? If they were frightened or got stuck halfway, then their master would light a fire in the grate below and force the boys to fight their way up—or die. Quite a few boys died that way. But who cared? Boys were cheap and nobody was prepared to fight for their rights.

Except for one man. He was the last person you'd think would bother about poor children. He was rich and came from a famous family. Other well-meaning people had murmured against putting children to work in such terrible conditions, but this man talked and wrote and talked again till he got Parliament to listen to him. Finally he succeeded. No more children were to be sent down the mines, work in the factories or be pushed up chimneys.

This man's name was Lord Shaftesbury and he went on helping poor children as long as he lived. He thought that the best possible thing for children was to go to school. You may not agree, of course! But coming to school is surely better than being pushed up a chimney, and having a fire lit beneath you.

Prayer

Dear Father God, thank you for those who work hard to teach us at school.

 **Suggested activity**

A chimney sweep's guide

Here is a picture of a well-to-do house. As you can see, there are lots of fireplaces for the chimney sweep to clean. All the chimneys connect with at least one other one. Some of them have fires lit in them, so they are no-go areas. The little sweep has to find his way from the basement to the top chimney without passing through a lit fireplace.

See how quickly you can do this.

Symbol

Suggested songs

There are hundreds of sparrows (JP246; K320; C202)
Just as the Father sent you, Lord (K223)

Reproduced with permission from *Stories of Everyday Saints* published by BRF 2002 (1 84101 224 6)

St Joseph

Key date: 1 May

Foster-father of Christ, husband of the Blessed Virgin Mary, patron of fathers of families and manual workers, especially carpenters.

Joseph was a good man.

MATTHEW 1:19

Joseph makes things happen

If it hadn't been for Joseph, baby Jesus might never have survived.

Joseph was a carpenter. He lived in a village called Nazareth and was doing well enough to marry. The girl he loved said 'Yes', so they got engaged. Then Joseph discovered that his beloved Mary was having a baby by someone else! Joseph was a good man and didn't want to shame her in front of everyone, so he decided to break off the engagement quietly. Then a great angel appeared to him in a dream, saying, 'Mary's baby has come from God. Go ahead and marry her.'

So Joseph did. He looked after Mary beautifully. Then the government said that everyone had to be counted in their home town on a certain date. So Joseph took Mary and travelled down to Bethlehem, the town his family came from. There was no room at the inn, and Mary was near the time for her to give birth. Trust Joseph to find somewhere for them to take shelter—even if it was only a stable at first. There the baby was born.

Baby Jesus and his mother had a strange mixture of visitors. Some were poor, like the shepherds. Some brought impressive gifts, like the wise men. Then, just as they were about to return home, the angel appeared to Joseph in his sleep again. 'Get up! Hurry! Take the child and his mother into Egypt and stay there till I tell you to return. The king is looking for the child to kill him.'

Joseph hurried them away. He had the tools of his trade with him. He could work. They would survive. They stayed in Egypt until it was safe to return, and then Joseph took his little family up to Nazareth to live. There he looked after Jesus and taught him all he knew. Baby Jesus would not have survived without Joseph's loving care.

Prayer

Dear Father God, look after me wherever I go, especially when I get into trouble.

Suggested activities

Think of a world without any trees or plants

How many of the things from this house are made of wood? How many are made from other plants?

Tree scramble

Can you unscramble the letters to reveal the names of British trees?

1. PLAPE
2. HAS
3. HECEB
4. CRIBH
5. RIF
6. ZEHAL
7. LYOHL
8. MILE
9. AKO
10. REAP
11. MULP
12. RANOW
13. MYCAROSE
14. NALTUW
15. LOWWIL
16. SHORE THUNCEST

Discuss what food we can get from trees (for example, apples, bananas, chocolate, coconuts, damsons, dates, lemons, maple syrup, nuts of all sorts, olives, oranges, pears, plums).

Carpenters were the craftsmen of the day. Not only did they make furniture, but also the forms or templates on which Roman arches and tunnels were based. They were well-paid and respected.

Symbol

Suggested songs
Away in a manger (JP12)
Mary's song (St S85)

(1. Apple 2. Ash 3. Beech 4. Birch 5. Fir 6. Hazel 7. Holly 8. Lime 9. Oak 10. Pear 11. Plum 12. Rowan 13. Sycamore 14. Walnut 15. Willow 16. Horse Chestnut)

Reproduced with permission from *Stories of Everyday Saints* published by BRF 2002 (1 84101 224 6)

St John the Apostle

Key date: 6 May

Died late 1st century.
Writer of the Gospel of
St John. Described in his
Gospel as 'the disciple
Jesus loved'. Patron saint
of writers.

God loved the people of this world so much
that he gave his only Son, so that everyone
who has faith in him will have eternal life
and never really die.

JOHN 3:16

The loyal friend

Do you have a nickname?

John and his brother James were so quick-tempered
that Jesus nicknamed them the Sons of Thunder. John
in particular was only a young man when he and James
left their father and the boats to follow Jesus. Along
with Peter and his brother Andrew, those two hotheads
were very close to Jesus. They watched him heal
people, they listened when he taught, they were at their
Last Supper together, and they were in the garden with
him afterwards.

When the soldiers came to arrest Jesus, his friends
ran away. John didn't go far away, though. Afterwards,
he followed wherever Jesus was taken. John was right
there with Jesus' mother when he was put up on the
cross to die. Jesus said to his mother, 'This man is now
your son.' And to John he said, 'She is now your
mother.' From that time on, John took Mary into his
own home.

John was one of the first to see Jesus when he rose
from the dead. Though it was Peter who became the
leader of Jesus' friends, John shared in all their ups and
downs, even being imprisoned with Peter for a while.
Peter was the spokesman but John had a special job to
do—two jobs, really. First he looked after Mary, taking
her away to live in Ephesus, in what is now Turkey. His
other job was to write down what he'd seen. He lived to
a great age and, looking back, he could see what was
most important in what Jesus had said and done. His
great themes were 'Love one another', and 'God loved
the world so much that he gave his only Son that
everyone who has faith in him will have eternal life and
never really die.'

Prayer

Dear Father, help me to be as loving to others as you
are to me.

Suggested activities

Friendly words

FOR YOUNGER CHILDREN

Think of something really nice to say to the person next to you. Then that person has to say something nice about the person next to them… and so on round the group.

Write about someone you like

FOR OLDER CHILDREN

Write a story or a poem describing someone or something you like very much. This could be someone in your family, or a pet. Make sure you tell us why you like them, and how you show that you like them.

Or write a poem in which the first letter in each line spells a person's name, such as:

*Mum is marvellous at
Understanding what it's like to be
Me.*

Symbol

Suggested songs

Jesus bids us shine (JP128)
Love your neighbour (S44)
A new commandment (C2)

Florence Nightingale

Key date: born 12 May

1820–1910.
Founder of trained nursing
as a profession for women.

The Spirit has given… the power to
heal the sick.

1 CORINTHIANS 12:9

The Lady with the Lamp

Sometimes God says that he's got a job for us but he doesn't make it clear what it is. This happened to Florence Nightingale. She came from a wealthy Victorian family but wasn't content to sit around and do nothing all day. When she was 17, she heard God saying that he had a special mission for her, but it was a long time before she realized what it was.

Florence didn't waste time, though. First she trained as a nurse and read everything she could about public health and hospitals. She became such an authority that even some members of the government listened to her.

War broke out in a part of Russia known as the Crimea. Florence got permission to go out there with six other nurses to look after the sick and wounded. What she found was truly horrifying! Men lay packed closely together on straw, with no running water to wash in, or even loos. Rats and fleas tormented them and even drinking water was rationed. Their so-called nurses were mostly drunk and disorderly.

Florence had raised some money to take with her. So what do you think was the first thing she ordered for her makeshift hospital? Two hundred scrubbing brushes!

Once the place was clean and the worst of the so-called nurses dismissed, she was able to tackle the real job of looking after the men—and the men got better as conditions improved.

Later, Florence helped to found St Thomas' Hospital to train nurses. But every night, back in the Crimea, she took her lamp and walked through the wards to see that all was well. The men looked out for her coming and that is how she became known as the Lady with the Lamp.

Prayer

Dear Lord, show me today how to help others who may be hurting in their bodies, or in their minds.

 **Suggested activities**

What's the matter?

Here are some pictures of children who feel unwell. Can you say what could be wrong with each one of them?

Going to hospital

Have you ever been to see a doctor at a hospital, or do you know someone who has? Write a story about what happened, why you or the other person went to hospital, and how the illness was cured.

Keeping healthy

Discuss what we need to keep us healthy—diet, exercise, sleep, hygiene and so on.

Symbol

Suggested songs

Jesus' hands were kind hands (JP134; K194)
God, you can use me (K89)

Reproduced with permission from *Stories of Everyday Saints* published by BRF 2002 (1 84101 224 6)

St Barnabas

Key date: 11 June

1st century.
Paul's sponsor and
companion on his
first journey.

**Barnabas helped him by taking him
to the apostles.**

ACTS 9:27

The team manager

After Jesus died, many of his friends fled from Jerusalem. Everywhere they went, they talked about Jesus. Some even talked about him to Gentiles—that is, people who were not Jews. This shocked the top people in Jerusalem because Jewish law said that Jews mustn't mix with Gentiles. So they sent a Cypriot called Barnabas to see what was going on.

Barnabas realized that everyone, everywhere—not just Jews—needed to hear about Jesus, but that it would take a special sort of man to make it happen. He himself was a big, strong man, but had he the right gifts for the job?

Barnabas didn't think he had. But he knew a man who could talk the hind leg off a donkey, a man who couldn't be beaten in an argument, a man who loved Jesus so much that he'd endured beatings for his sake. Barnabas went in search of this man and, when he'd found him, got him to agree that they should work together. They made a powerful team, travelling by land and by sea, talking about Jesus wherever they went.

Soon Barnabas found that his friend outshone him, but Barnabas didn't mind that. The great thing was that together they were carrying the news about Jesus far and wide. They had many fantastic adventures, and they quarrelled and parted, only to make up later on.

If Barnabas hadn't gone looking for this man, we might never have heard about a saint called Paul, who took the words of Jesus out into the great world, far beyond the lands Barnabas knew. Barnabas was a wise man. He realized that sometimes the most important thing you can do is to encourage someone else to do the job even better than you can. The name Barnabas means 'encourager'.

Prayer

Dear Lord Jesus, help me to encourage other people to do their best.

 # Suggested activities

Be an encourager!

Write a description of your best friend in four words, saying only nice things. For example, you could say that he or she was brave, sporty and good fun… or kind, pretty, loyal and sympathetic.

Suggested songs

What a friend we have in Jesus (JP273)
It's a fact that you can share a smile (S71)

Symbol

This can also be done with everyone sitting in a circle. Each person takes it in turn to say something nice about the person sitting next to them. This can be physical—for instance, that they have lovely hair—or about their nature— for instance, that they are quick to help out at home if something needs to be done.

Make a boat for Barnabas

You'll find the instructions on pages 95–96.

Reproduced with permission from *Stories of Everyday Saints* published by BRF 2002 (1 84101 224 6)

    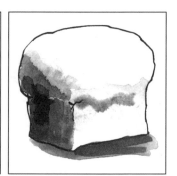

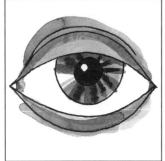   

   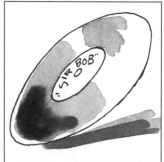

St Alban

Key date: 22 June

3rd-century Roman citizen who changed cloaks with a fugitive Christian priest and was beheaded in his place.

He will take the punishment for... others.

ISAIAH 53:11

The man in the hooded cloak

Nowadays, you don't get arrested and killed just because you're a Christian—not in most countries, anyway. But this did happen when the Romans ruled Britain. Alban was a retired soldier and knew exactly what happened to Christians who were caught. But he wasn't a Christian, so he wasn't in danger, was he?

Then came a frantic knocking on his door. A man in a long hooded cloak stood there, begging for help. 'Soldiers! After me! I'm a Christian! Please, hide me till they've gone by!'

It would have been safest to slam the door in the man's face. But Alban let him in. Why? Because he was curious to hear about this Jesus for whom Christians risked death.

Over the next few days, Alban heard about the wonderful things Jesus had said and done. He watched his guest worshipping and praying. Alban realized that what he'd been missing in his own life was the love of Jesus, so he became a Christian, too.

The only thing was, someone gave them away and the soldiers came pounding on the door.

'Quick!' said Alban. 'Give me your old cloak! You take mine, and slip out the back way.'

Alban pulled the hood of the cloak over his head and was led before the judge, who recognized him.

'Come, my friend,' said the judge. 'Sacrifice to our Roman gods and we'll say no more about your helping a criminal to escape.'

Alban refused, so the soldiers led him out of town and up a small hill covered with wild flowers. Alban knelt and with one blow his head was cut off.

Alban's death caused such a stir that soon the laws against Christians were relaxed and people could worship Jesus openly again.

Prayer

Dear Lord Jesus, help me to stand firm in my love for you, even when others don't share it and perhaps even laugh at me because of it.

 ## Suggested activities

Changing clothes

You will need:
- Photocopies of the drawings opposite
- Thin card
- Glue or paper paste
- Scissors
- Crayons

Slit   Slits   Slit

Colour in the two men opposite, cut them out and paste on to thin card.

Colour in and cut out the two cloaks, with tabs. Carefully cut slits where shown, and push tabs through slits.

As the story is told, the characters exchange cloaks.

Symbol

Search for the words

Find the words in the grid.

M	X	S	O	L	D	I	E	R	S	J
P	A	L	B	A	N	E	W	G	H	E
E	V	G	I	H	X	C	R	O	S	S
S	Q	U	I	D	L	I	D	Y	R	U
U	C	L	M	S	N	F	O	Q	O	S
O	L	X	Z	A	T	I	O	J	R	S
H	O	O	D	I	X	R	R	Z	E	W
W	A	Q	U	N	R	C	A	V	P	O
Y	K	B	G	T	Z	A	P	T	M	R
F	L	O	W	E	R	S	E	Y	E	D

Alban
hood
cloak
house
cross
Jesus
door
magistrate
emperor
saint
eyes
sacrifice
flowers
soldiers
hill
sword

Suggested song

Be bold, be strong (JP14; K17)

Reproduced with permission from *Stories of Everyday Saints* published by BRF 2002 (1 84101 224 6)

St Peter

Key date: 29 June

1st century, died about AD64. Jesus' right-hand man and leader of the Christian Church after his death.

Jesus asked… 'Simon son of John, do you love me?' Peter answered, 'Yes, Lord, you know I love you!' 'Then take care of my sheep.'

JOHN 21:16

The right-hand man

Have you ever done anything really bad? So bad that when you think about it, you go hot and cold all over? Peter did just that.

Simon Peter was married and making a good living as a fisherman when Jesus called him to be a fisher of people instead. Peter became leader of the twelve friends who followed Jesus. He was Jesus' right-hand man and was always there, through bad times and good. He saw the miracles Jesus did, and he remembered everything that happened, so that later it could be written down for people to read about.

Peter had great faith, but great failings, too. He told Jesus that he was prepared to die for him, but within hours—when he was questioned by Jesus' enemies—Peter denied that he even knew him. Jesus forgave Peter because he saw how sorry he was, and Peter was one of the first people Jesus appeared to after he rose from the dead.

Jesus told Peter, 'Take care of my sheep.' He meant that Peter was to look after all those who loved Jesus, like a shepherd.

Jesus also said that Peter would hold the keys to the kingdom of heaven, which is why he's often pictured holding two large keys.

Peter wasn't perfect. He made crashing mistakes. But he had also had the insight to understand that Jesus was the Son of God before anyone else did. He had a warm heart and a quick temper. Men like that may make mistakes, but when they learn by their mistakes, they become great leaders. Just as Jesus had said he would, Peter became the leader of Jesus' friends after his death and helped to spread the good news far and wide.

Prayer

Dear Lord Jesus, you know that I often do wrong and silly things. Please forgive me, and help me to see where I can make up for my mistakes.

Suggested activities
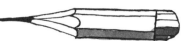

Hunt for the keyholes

See how many things you can find in this picture which need a key to start or open them.

Different sorts of keys

Discuss what other forms a key can take—for example, credit cards, swipe cards for money or for access, codes and ciphers, piano keys, computer keys.

Key code

Below is a simple coded message in which letters are represented by numbers. For instance, 1 = S, 2 = E, 3 = T and 4 = A. With these to give you a start, can you work out what the message is?

3 4 5 2   6 4 7 2   8 9

10 11   1 12 2 2 13

Answer: Take care of my sheep

Symbol

Suggested songs

Silver and gold (JP198; K281)
Big man (JP16)
I will make you fishers of men (JP123)
Where are you going? (ST S69)
Fisherman Peter on the sea (S34)

Reproduced with permission from *Stories of Everyday Saints* published by BRF 2002 (1 84101 224 6)

St Paul

Christ… sent me to tell the good news.

1 CORINTHIANS 1:17

Little man, big voice

Paul hated Christians. He hunted them down and dragged them off to prison. He thought he was doing God's work—until one day, on his way to arrest some more Christians, he had a vision from God and understood that he'd got it all wrong. The people he'd been hunting were really God's friends, and Jesus was the Son of God.

After Paul worked out where he'd gone wrong, he was as eager to talk about Jesus as he'd been against him before. His former friends were furious with Paul. They tried everything they could think of to stop him talking about Jesus. He was beaten up, put in prison, beaten again. He walked with a stick after a time, and limped a bit. But that didn't stop him. Up and down the Mediterranean he went, getting on and off boats, talking, talking… working at the leather trade to keep himself… making friends, making enemies.

Paul knew how to tell the story of Jesus so that people would understand. He had the most marvellous adventures. In one place, he healed a poor mad girl, and everyone thought he was a Roman 'god' and wanted to worship him! In another, he was thrown into a deep dungeon in chains—until an earthquake set him free. If Paul was on a ship and it got wrecked and sank, Paul would be certain to bob up again, probably still talking. He came from what is now Turkey, where they laugh and sing and fight a lot. Paul could do all of those things and do them well. But its the letters he wrote to tell people about Jesus that made the greatest impact. Many of his adventures were written down by his friend, Doctor Luke, and we can read about them in the Acts of the Apostles.

Prayer

Dear Lord Jesus, help me to talk about you as my friend, just as Paul did.

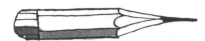 

Suggested activities

Where did Paul go?

On the map given below of the Mediterranean, trace the journeys Paul took, ending up in Rome.

A great adventure

Write a story about a shipwreck in which you were saved. Was the ship sunk in a storm, crashed on to a rock, or sunk in a battle? How did you get ashore? On a raft, by swimming, with a rope thrown from land, or on a lifeboat?

Symbol

If you landed alone on a desert island, what would you eat, and how would you make a shelter?

Suggested songs

Alleluia, alleluia, give thanks to the risen Lord (JP3)
Never-ending love (S67)
Paul: take heart, my friends (St S68)
Here is the news (S89)

Bob Geldof, KMG

(Knight of the Order of St Michael and St George)

To everyone who is thirsty, he gives something to drink; to everyone who is hungry, he gives good things to eat.

PSALM 107:9

Band Aid

The pop singer was feeling sorry for himself. Nobody seemed interested in the records he was making. He switched on the television and saw something that put his own troubles into the shade. What he saw were the pictures of starving children in Ethiopia.

He couldn't get them out of his mind. Shrunken children with enormous eyes, tottering after a lorry which might—perhaps—contain food. What could he do about it? He could send money, of course. But was that enough? He could, perhaps, make a record and give the profits from it.

He started asking people in the music business to help. They said yes, he ought to do it, and yes, they would help. In one day he went from thinking that 'someone' ought to do 'something' to organizing all the top bands in the country to make a record. Now and then he wondered how he dared. But he couldn't stop. He just had to do it! He got the record company, the artist for the cover, the recording studio, and the most famous pop stars in the country.

On the morning the record was to be made, he had no idea how many people would turn up. They'd promised to come, but would they really give up their time to do it? For free?

But they came. And they sang 'Do They Know It's Christmas?' which went straight to the top of the charts and is still being sung today. All the money went to the project called Band Aid. Later, Bob Geldof managed to organize a worldwide 24-hour concert called Live Aid, including artists from all round the world.

God used Bob Geldof to arrange for aid to be poured into Africa to help the starving children.

Prayer

Dear Lord Jesus, never let me forget that I, too, can do something to help to feed children who have nothing to eat or drink.

Suggested activities

Do They Know It's Christmas?

Teach the children this song.

Fund-raisers!

Brainstorm all the things you could do together to raise money to help children who don't have enough to eat or drink. Hold a fund-raising event for a children's charity.

Quote from 'Is That It?' by Bob Geldof (slightly edited)

'God came down from heaven to find someone to alert the world to the holocaust which was sweeping Africa. He knocked at the wrong door. It was answered by Bob Geldof. "Who's he?" thought God. "Oh, never mind, he'll do."'

Do you think God knocked at the wrong door by mistake and, when it was opened by this scruffy Irishman, thought, 'Oh well—he'll do'?

NB: As Bob Geldof is an Irish citizen, his proper title is 'Bob Geldof, KMG' and not 'Sir Bob Geldof'.

Symbol

Suggested songs

'Do They Know It's Christmas?' is included in *Christmas Singalong*, Music Sales. Also available on single sheet IMP Code 9783.
Small things count (S81)

Reproduced with permission from *Stories of Everyday Saints* published by BRF 2002 (1 84101 224 6)

John Newton

**Key date:
24 July**

1725–1807.
Once a slave
trader, on his
conversion he
worked to abolish
slavery. Later he
became a
clergyman and
wrote the hymn
'Amazing Grace'.

**But God treats us much better than we
deserve, and because of Christ Jesus, he
freely accepts us and sets us free from
our sins.**

ROMANS 3:24

The slave trader

John was a bright lad and expected to do well. True, his
mother had died when he was seven, but at eleven he
went to sea with his father and loved it. He had amazing
adventures, being lucky to escape with his life several
times. Then he became reckless and began to get into
trouble all the time. His father despaired. Hadn't John
been brought up a Christian? But John had turned his
back on Jesus.

He deserted from the Navy, but was caught and
flogged. For over a year he was at the mercy of a slave
dealer in Africa, who treated him very badly. The only
bright spot in his life was the memory of a girl called
Mary, whom he'd met when she was only 13. But Mary
seemed very far away then.

John managed to get a job back at sea, but one
stormy night his luck completely deserted him. The
ship he was steering was waterlogged and sinking. He
had been reading about God's love for those who do
bad things. Facing death, he promised that if he lived,
he would mend his ways.

He survived and became captain of a slave ship.
Hardly anyone saw anything wrong in that. It was the
Africans who captured and sold their own people,
wasn't it? There was nothing new about keeping slaves,
was there? But John continued to read the Bible and
made friends with people who thought differently. He
left the sea, married his Mary and began to work with
his new friends to abolish the slave trade. After some
years, he was ordained and became as good and great a
man as he had been bad before. Today we remember
him because he wrote the hymn 'Amazing Grace'.

Prayer

Dear Lord Jesus, help me to turn away from the bad
things in my life and look for your forgiveness.

Suggested activity

Symbol

FOR ALL AGES

Saying sorry

Write a poem or a short story about someone doing something bad, and then being sorry for it.

Suggested song

Amazing grace (JP8; K9)

Reproduced with permission from *Stories of Everyday Saints* published by BRF 2002 (1 84101 224 6)

St Christopher

Key date: 25 July

3rd century.
The patron saint of
travellers, who used his great
strength to carry people over
a river. One day he carried
the Christ-child himself.

Love the Lord your God with all your heart,
soul, and strength.

DEUTERONOMY 6:5

The strong man

Do you admire strong people?

This story is about a big, strong man who loved Jesus. He wasn't clever. He couldn't read or write or do sums. He desperately wanted to serve Jesus, but he didn't know how.

He lived near a wide, shallow river. There was no bridge over the river, or even a boat to ferry people across. If they wanted to go from one side to the other, they had to wade through, and sometimes they fell in!

So this man had an idea. He would use his great strength to serve others by carrying them across the river. He built himself a hut on the bank and soon he was a familiar sight, wading through the water, carrying people on his back.

One dark and stormy night, the river ran dangerously fast. The man was just thinking how glad he was that no one would need him when there came a knock on the door. A child stood there.

'Will you carry me over the water?'

With a sigh, the man took his staff in his hand, bent down to let the child climb on his back and waded into the river.

At first the child was light and all the man had to struggle with was the rush of the water and the thrashing of the wind and rain. But halfway across, the child grew heavier… and heavier… until it was all the man could do to stagger to the far bank and set his burden down.

'You are the heaviest weight I have ever carried,' he said.

The child replied, 'That is because I bear the sins of the world. Since you have looked after the weak and carried the Christ-child on your back, you shall now be called Christ-bearer, or Christopher.'

That is why Christopher is the special saint for travellers.

Prayer

Dear Lord God, let me use whatever gifts you have given me, to serve you.

 **Suggested activities**

Stepping stones

This is a variant of musical chairs. Supply as many sheets of newspaper as there are children, minus one. The floor is now a river, and the children can only cross it on the paper 'stones'. Only one child can safely stand on each piece of paper at a time. Play some music and, when it stops, the children must find themselves a new piece of paper. One child will be left out. Remove one or two pieces of paper until there is only one piece left.

The strongest man in the world

Do you know the name of the strongest man in the world today? How much can he lift at any one time? You can find out who he is by looking in the *Guinness Book of Records*—there should be a copy in your local library.

Tug-of-war

This is a playground activity which must be properly supervised. A rope needs to be supplied, and care taken that the two sides are roughly equal in strength. Have a tug-of-war: which side is the stronger?

Symbol

How do you cross the river?

Draw a river and some people standing on the bank. There is no bridge. Draw at least two ways in which they might cross the river without building a bridge.

Here are some ideas to start you off: stepping stones, a ford, riding a horse, swinging across on a rope, by boat, chain-ferry or helicopter.

Suggested songs

My God is so big (JP169; K255)
My God is so great (C169)

Reproduced with permission from *Stories of Everyday Saints* published by BRF 2002 (1 84101 224 6)

Mother Teresa

Key date: 27 August

1910–1997
The little nun who founded the Missionaries of Charity, begun in India but eventually worldwide. Nobel Peace Prize winner.

'When I was hungry, you gave me something to eat, and when I was thirsty, you gave me something to drink. When I was a stranger, you welcomed me, and when I was naked, you gave me clothes to wear.'

MATTHEW 25:35–36

Mother Teresa of Calcutta

Mother Teresa was a little woman with the biggest heart you could find. Born in Albania to wealthy parents, she wanted nothing more than to work in India. Joining a Catholic sisterhood, she took the name of Teresa and went to teach in a rich girls' school in Calcutta. But this didn't satisfy her. While travelling on a train to Darjeeling, she heard God's voice telling her to reach out to the poorest of the poor. But how? What could she do? She had no money, and no one would look after her if she left the safety of the wealthy school and went out into the streets on her own.

But that is just what she did. She prayed about it. Then she bought the cheapest sari she could find, and set off into the poorest quarters of Calcutta. For the first time she saw terrible poverty and lack of care for the sick and dying. At first she was on her own, doing what she could. It was then that she discovered the power of persistent prayer. People didn't particularly want to give her medicines, food and money, but somehow they always ended up doing so.

Soon seven sisters joined her, then a hundred, and by 1997 she had a thousand! She started schools, opened orphanages and hospices—not only in India, but wherever there was a need, all over the world. Governments fell over themselves to help her. The Pope gave her a beautiful car, which she sold to fund a new house. She was given the Nobel Peace Prize, and asked that the money usually spent on the prizegiving ceremony be given to the poor instead.

Her life shows how much someone who believes in persistent prayer can achieve.

Prayer

Dear Father God, show me how to serve others.

Suggested activity

What is a hospice?

FOR ALL AGES

The word 'hospice' means a travellers' house of rest, or a home for the poor and the sick. Nowadays, it usually refers to special places that look after people who are dying. Talk about hospices, especially about hospices for children in your area. Perhaps arrange for someone from a hospice to visit your children. Arrange a fundraising day for a hospice, to buy something they particularly need.

Symbol

Suggested songs

When I needed a neighbour (JP275; C229)
Jesus' hands were kind hands (JP134; K194)
I sing a song of the saints (JP115)

Reproduced with permission from *Stories of Everyday Saints* published by BRF 2002 (1 84101 224 6)

John Bunyan

Key date: 31 August

1628–1688.
The tinker turned preacher who wrote
The Pilgrim's Progress in Bedford gaol.

**I am here in prison for preaching
the good news.**

PHILEMON 13

A Pilgrim's Progress

Do you like making a lot of noise? Do you like playing football?

John Bunyan did both. His father had a good business mending pots and pans, but John ran away to serve in the army. When he returned home, he married and tried to settle down. He thought of himself as a good sort of man, but every other word was a swear word.

Then his wife died and he realized that he was not a good man at all, but a poor sort of creature pretending to be good. He began to understand that God really loved him. He stopped swearing and started telling other people what he'd learned about God. He found he could talk well and many people—especially the poor—came to listen when he spoke informally in the fields outside towns.

This didn't please the ministers in the Church. They said, 'Who is this swearing tinker? What right has he to preach to people who should be listening to us?' So they tried to stop him.

John was put in Bedford gaol for three months. They said, 'You can leave any time after that if you promise to stop preaching.' John wouldn't promise, so he stayed in gaol for twelve years. To feed his family, he made long-tagged laces, which he sold to pedlars. While he was in prison, he wrote some brilliant adventure stories.

His best-known book is *The Pilgrim's Progress*. A pilgrim is a man on a journey to a holy place. The hero in this book is called Christian. He meets giants and a dragon, castles and lions; there are villains who try to harm him, and people who help him through. It's as exciting a story today as when it was written so many years ago.

Prayer

Dear Lord Jesus, please help me to put my bad habits, like swearing, behind me.

 **Suggested activities**

Make a frieze

Make a frieze showing *The Pilgrim's Progress*. Here are some of the events that could be drawn or painted:

- ✪ Christian, with a load on his back, being pulled out of the swamp by Mr Help.
- ✪ Christian walks between two fierce lions to reach the palace in safety.
- ✪ Christian, wearing medieval armour, fights the fierce dragon.
- ✪ Christian weaves his way through the alleys of Vanity town to reach the truth.
- ✪ Christian in the dungeon of Giant Despair's Doubting Castle.
- ✪ Christian crosses the last river. All the trumpets sound for him on the other side.

Strip cartoon

Make a strip cartoon.
- ✪ Decide how many frames are needed to tell the story.
- ✪ Decide what the characters look like and how they are dressed.

You can tell the story in ruled-off spaces at the top or bottom of the pictures, and/or you can tell the story in speech bubbles. There should be no more than two speech bubbles in each frame. The top left bubble reads first, the bottom right second.

Children's versions of *The Pilgrim's Progress* are available as follows:

The Pilgrim's Progress by Geraldine McCaughrean, ill. Jason Cockcroft, published by Hodder Children's Books. This book won the Blue Peter Book Award 2000. There is also a smaller paperback version.

The Pilgrim's Progress by Alan and Linda Parry, John Hunt Publishers.

Symbol

Suggested songs

He who would valiant be (To be a pilgrim) (JP80)
One more step (JP188; C166; K273; S94)
Keep me close to you (K224)

Reproduced with permission from *Stories of Everyday Saints* published by BRF 2002 (1 84101 224 6)

St Hildegard of Bingen

Key date: 17 September

Musician, artist, naturalist and visionary. Influential Benedictine abbess in Germany.

I will praise you, Lord! You always do right.
I will sing about you, the Lord Most High.

PSALM 7:17

The singer at work

Singing came as easily to Hildegard as talking does to other people, but she wasn't a pop star. She was a busy woman with a large convent of nuns to look after. She had the knack of looking after people. She didn't let them get away with anything stupid, mind you. But you really did not want to behave badly when she was around.

From the time that she was a little child, Hildegard was very aware of God—not all the time, but enough times to know that she wanted to serve him always. Now she was grown up and in charge of other people, she found that there were lots of ways she could serve God. For one thing, she could make up songs in praise of him.

God had given Hildegard many different talents and she tried to use them all. Born into a noble family, she'd been well educated and she loved books. She loved the beauty of the world around her, so she wrote a book about the plants, the trees, the animals, the fishes— everything that she saw around her in the world that God made.

She also studied medicine. Perhaps today she would have been a doctor. In those days she looked after the sick people in the convent, and wrote another book about medicine. She also loved to hear about the people whom God had used to be his hands and feet in the world, so she wrote a book about them, too.

And all the time she sang. She didn't sing other people's songs, but made up her own. Some of her songs have been recorded recently and now we can hear again the praises she sang to the Lord, all those years ago.

Prayer

Dear Lord, show me how best to use the gifts you have given me.

 **Suggested activities**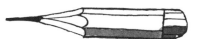

Hunt the herb

In medieval times, the gardens of abbeys were like Kew Gardens and Wisley today. They were the places where you would find all the latest plants. The gardeners there were not interested in flowers for their beauty, but in plants which would provide herbs and vegetables for cooking and for medicinal purposes. There were no firms supplying medicines then, so instead the abbeys used a variety of plants—sometimes with surprising results!

In the countryside today we still look for a dock leaf to soothe the skin if we are unlucky enough to brush against a stinging nettle. And if we need to feed a caged bird, we still look for chickweed.

Here are pictures of different herbs that are widely used in cooking nowadays. Can you put the right name to each of them?

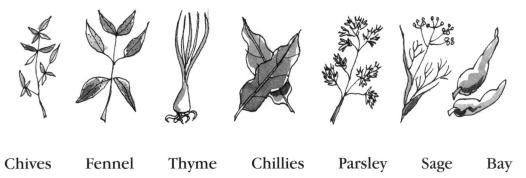

Chives   Fennel   Thyme   Chillies   Parsley   Sage   Bay

Draw a herb

Show the children some of the common herbs and ask them if they know what they are used for in cooking. Then ask them to draw at least one so that they will recognize it in future.

Symbol

Suggested songs

Praise him, praise him, praise him in the morning (JP202; C177)
Praise him on the trumpet (JP200; K284)

CDs of Hildegard's music are available as follows:
A Feather on the Breath of God, sequences and hymns by Hildegard of Bingen. Performed by 'Gothic Voices' with Emma Kirkby, Hyperion CD 66039. This CD won a Gramophone Record Award.
Vision—the music of Hildegard of Bingen, HMV classics, HMV 5735472.
Canticles of Ecstasy, the music of Hildegard von Bingen, Sequentia 05472773202.

St Michael

Key date: 29 September

Archangel, and commander-in-chief of the forces of good against evil. Guardian angel of the Hebrew nation.

A war broke out in heaven. Michael and his angels were fighting against the dragon and its angels. But the dragon lost the battle. It and its angels were forced out of their places in heaven and were thrown down to the earth.

REVELATION 12:7–9

The commander-in-chief

The story goes like this. God ruled over his angels in heaven long before our earth was formed. It was a time of golden peace. The archangels were the mightiest of all the angels, shining with the reflected light of God. One of these great archangels—called Lucifer—was indeed strong and handsome, but also very vain. Lucifer forgot that his mighty powers came from God and boasted that no one was greater than he. In time he began to think that he was as great as God himself.

'I am the greatest! There is no one who can outshine me in my glory! Not even God can touch me!'

This made God very sad. God is love, and he's always sad when his creatures turn away from him.

Lucifer gathered together a small following of lesser angels who feared him. Finally he announced that he was going to take God's throne for himself. It was war in heaven.

The command of the forces of the light was given to the great archangel Michael, who put on the armour God had given him and prepared his forces for the battle. He told his followers, 'Lucifer has become an evil dragon, and must be destroyed.' Michael and his angels defeated Lucifer and cast him out of heaven and down to earth.

Now Lucifer stalks about the earth, pouring poison into the ears of whoever will listen to him. But Michael is always on the watch to defeat him. Remember that God is mightier than all the angels put together, and evil succeeds on earth only when we allow it to do so. There are many churches and high places named after Michael, particularly Mont St Michel in Brittany and St Michael's Mount in Cornwall.

Prayer

Dear loving Father, help me always to fight on the side of right and light.

 **Suggested activities**

Dragons

Here are some pictures of animals that look like dragons. Photocopy them on to stiff paper. Colour them in and cut them out to mount on a frieze on the wall.

What do we need to fight evil?

Michael put on the armour of God. St Paul explained that each piece of armour is given to us by God to help us fight evil. This is what he said:

Be ready! Let the truth be like a belt around your waist, and let God's justice protect you like armour. Your desire to tell the good news about peace should be like shoes on your feet. Let your faith be like a shield, and you will be able to stop all the flaming arrows of the evil one. Let God's saving power be like a helmet, and for a sword use God's message that comes from the Spirit.

EPHESIANS 6:14–17

Discuss what the children perceive as evil today, and what they can do about it.

Symbol

Suggested songs

I may never march in the infantry (JP101)
I am a soldier in the army of the Lord (K116)

Reproduced with permission from *Stories of Everyday Saints* published by BRF 2002 (1 84101 224 6)

St Francis of Assisi

**Key date:
4 October**

1181–1226.
Founder of
Franciscan order,
patron of natural
conservation.
Originator of
nativity cribs.
Received the marks
corresponding to
Christ's wounds on
his own body.

Jesus said, 'Put your finger here and look
at my hands!'

JOHN 20:27

The man who talked to the birds

Francis was born with a silver spoon in his mouth. He was the original spoilt rich kid on the block. But he was deeply unhappy. He went into a tumbledown little church, got down on his knees and asked God what he was to do.

'Rebuild my Church,' came the reply. 'You can see it is in a bad way.'

Francis looked around, and yes, he could see that the little church was in need of repair. He didn't for a minute suspect that God wanted him to tackle the problems of the worldwide Church. He just got on with the job of putting that one little building to rights. When he'd finished, he found that he was a penniless beggar, so he started going around preaching the love of God. He was a brilliant preacher! He could talk birds off the trees and a fierce wolf into lying at his feet.

Some friends joined him and the money came rolling in.

Francis said 'No' to the money. He wanted to be like Jesus, working for the poor and keeping nothing but the barest essentials for himself. His fame spread and the numbers of his followers—now called Franciscans—grew. And so did their influence. Francis loved Jesus so much that after a while his hands and feet showed the same wounds that Jesus received when he was nailed to the cross.

Francis taught a simple lifestyle and love of Jesus. This disturbed the Pope and the high and mighty bishops. At last they, too, began to think more about how they could help the poor, and less about counting their gold and silver.

Francis had done what God had asked of him. He had rebuilt God's Church—one step at a time.

Prayer

Dear Lord Jesus, show me how to do what is right, one step at a time.

Suggested activities

Francis and the birds

FOR YOUNGER CHILDREN

Draw and paint a picture (or make a collage) of birds all listening to Francis as he talks to them. A wolf should lie at his feet. Francis wears a brown or grey habit, corded at the waist.

FOR OLDER CHILDREN

Churches collage

Make a collage of different church buildings and cathedrals. This can be done with pictures either cut from magazines and newspapers, or drawn and painted. Some churches could have spires, others towers. Some of the churches might be from other parts of the world. If so, label them clearly.

FOR ALL AGES

Make a nativity set for Advent

Francis was the first to reconstruct a life-sized nativity in a grotto, using real animals. You will find instructions for making your own nativity set in Appendix One on page 90.

Suggested songs

Make me a channel of your peace
(JP161; K248; C152)
Canticle of the sun (St S2)
Rise, repair my church today! (St S55)
One more step along the world I go (JP188; K273; C166)

Symbol

Reproduced with permission from *Stories of Everyday Saints* published by BRF 2002 (1 84101 224 6)

St Luke

Key date: 18 October

The Greek doctor who kept Paul on the road. Author of the Acts of the Apostles and the Gospel that bears his name. Patron saint of doctors and artists.

Our dear doctor Luke sends you his greetings.

COLOSSIANS 4:14

The reporter

When did you last visit the doctor? Are you a good patient?

St Paul wore himself out travelling around the Mediterranean to tell people about Jesus. One day he was so ill that a Greek doctor called Luke was called in to treat him. Luke managed to get his patient back on his feet, and agreed to accompany Paul on his travels to look after him. Paul needed some looking after. I don't think he can have been a very good patient. He was always struggling to get out of bed before he was well enough.

Besides being a good doctor and, some say, a talented artist, Luke had a gift with words. He began to write an account for his Greek friends of the extraordinary things that he saw happen to Paul and his companions. What a lot there was to report! Riots, arrests, shipwrecks, miracles of healing; wicked people being struck blind, earthquakes: you name it, it happened to Paul.

So although Luke's first job was to look after Paul, it turned out that he had a second important task to perform—to write his story. Time has shown that Luke was an accurate reporter of the things he saw. His book might have been called *The Adventures of Paul*, but it's known today as the Acts of the Apostles. 'Apostle' is the Greek word for someone sent to do a special job for Jesus.

When Paul didn't need him, Luke travelled around gathering first-hand information about Jesus' life, death and resurrection. He even managed to get an account of Jesus' birth from his mother, Mary. Luke wrote all that down, too, in a book which is now known as the Gospel of St Luke.

Prayer

Dear Father God, help me always to tell the truth.

Suggested activities

Draw baby Jesus

Luke is said to have been an artist who drew and painted Jesus in the arms of his mother. Draw or paint baby Jesus in the arms of his mother.

Would you make a good reporter?

See Appendix Two on page 91, which gives suggestions about making your own newspaper with a group.

The memory game

A good reporter needs to be able to observe and report what he or she has seen.

You will need a tray with about fifteen different objects on it—for example: pen, pencil, rubber, book, spectacles, ball, spoon, thimble, scissors, clock, a glove and so on.

Symbol

Let the children have a minute to memorize the contents, then remove the tray and objects. The children now have to write down how many objects they can remember.

The winged bull refers to one of the four beasts surrounding the throne of God in Ezekiel (1:5–14), who are understood to be the four evangelists. There is also a reference to sacrifice in the temple in chapter l of Luke's Gospel.

Suggested songs

I sing a song of the saints (JP115)
Here is the news (S89)
Go, tell it on the mountain (JP65; C250)

Reproduced with permission from *Stories of Everyday Saints* published by BRF 2002 (1 84101 224 6)

St Frideswide

(pronounced 'Freedeswider')

**Key date:
19 October**

c.680–727.
The daughter of a
minor king, she fled
from the powerful
king of Mercia
through the forest. He
was temporarily
blinded but recovered
due to her prayers.

Be kind and tender-hearted to one another,
and forgive one another, as God has
forgiven you through Christ.

EPHESIANS 4:32 (GNB)

The beautiful princess

Do you find it hard to forgive someone who has hurt you? Once there was a beautiful princess called Frideswide. She was the daughter of a king who ruled over a small area to the west of Oxford. She loved God and wanted to spend her life serving him, but one day she was spotted by a very important man who wanted her to love him instead.

The princess said, 'No, thank you.' Unfortunately Aethelbald (Ethel-bald) wasn't the sort of man it was safe to say 'No' to. He was, in fact, the king of Mercia, and the princess's father was a king only because Aethelbald supported him. You can see the problem, both for the princess and for her father. If she kept on refusing Aethelbald, what would happen to them?

Bravely, Frideswide continued to say 'No' but she was frightened for herself and for her father, so she fled to a forest retreat to get away from Aethelbald.

Aethelbald was furious. He wasn't going to give her up. He pursued her into the forest. She doubled this way and that to elude him. Still he tracked her through the trees. Eventually she reached sanctuary in the little town of Oxford.

She was safe at last. But for Aethelbald, things could never be the same again, because on the last leg of his pursuit he was struck blind. Now he was sorry. He realized what a terrible thing he'd tried to do. He begged Frideswide to forgive him.

Could she manage to forgive him, in spite of what he'd tried to do? Well, she did. What's more, she even brought herself to pray that her persecutor might be healed. Aethelbald recovered his sight and Frideswide was able to devote her life to serving God.

Prayer

Dear Lord Jesus, help me to forgive those who hurt me.

 **Suggested activities**

Find the way for Frideswide

Find a way through the maze for Frideswide, so that she can reach Oxford in safety. And then find a way through the maze to a glade where Aethelbald is struck blind.

The important rule

Read this important message by jotting down every other letter in turn, starting with the F.

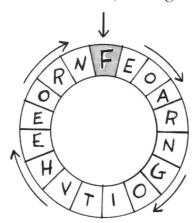

_ _ _ _ _ _ _   _ _ _   _ _ _ _ _ _ _

Symbol

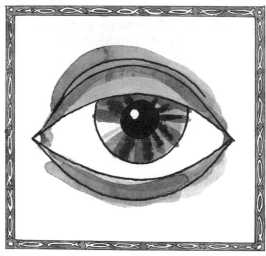

Reproduced with permission from *Stories of Everyday Saints* published by BRF 2002 (1 84101 224 6)

St Crispin and St Crispianus

**Key date:
25 October**

Died 285.
The Italian
shoemakers who
spread the good
news in
northern France.
They charged a
fair price to the
rich, but
attended the
poor for free.

**We struggled to make a living, so that we
could tell you God's message without being
a burden to anyone.**

1 Thessalonians 2:9

The shoemakers

Crispin and his brother were Christians at a time when
it wasn't a good idea to talk openly about Jesus.

'Be careful!' their friends said. 'You never know
who may be listening and might betray you to the
authorities.'

When it became too dangerous for them to stay in
Rome, the brothers worked their way up through Italy
and into northern France. They were shoemakers, and
there's always a need for people who can make and
repair shoes. They were true craftsmen and took pride
in their work. They bought good leather from the
tannery. They cut and shaped and stitched and
produced lightweight shoes for indoor use. They made
sandals for fine weather, and fitted leather uppers on to
wooden soles for use in wet weather. Sometimes they
hammered nails into the bottom of the wooden soles,
to make extra hard-wearing shoes and boots.

They would charge the rich a fair price, but they
didn't charge the poorest people at all. As you can
imagine, that made them very popular!

While they worked at their craft, Crispin and
Crispianus talked about Jesus, and after they'd put up
their shutters for the night they were often invited into
their customers' houses to pass on the stories they'd
heard about Jesus. They took pride in never asking
anyone for money to support them but, like St Paul,
they earned their living wherever they went.

Unfortunately, the Roman governor of the area
hated Christians and had forbidden anyone to speak the
name of Jesus. Crispin and his brother knew this, but
they went on spreading the good news… until one day
the soldiers caught up with them and they were killed.
But to this day, we remember that Christianity was
spread through northern France by two shoemakers.

Prayer

*Dear Father God, give us courage to talk to people
about you.*

Suggested activities

Footprints

You will need:
- Paper
- Pens
- Scissors

Nowadays, most people buy their shoes ready-made, but in earlier times, shoes were made to measure so that they fitted beautifully.

Make a collage. Every child draws round one of their shoes, cuts out the foot shape, and writes their name on it. These footprints can be stuck on a large sheet, overlapping one another, to make a pattern.

Name those shoes

Ask the children how many different types of shoes they can name—for example, trainers, boots, wellies, pumps, stilettos, court shoes, sandals, mules, slippers, galoshes, clogs.

What are shoes made of? For example, leather, plastic, cork, wood.

Symbol

Suggested song

God's not dead (No!) (JP60; K85; C72; K85)

Reproduced with permission from *Stories of Everyday Saints* published by BRF 2002 (1 84101 224 6)

St Winefride

Jesus answered, 'Everyone who drinks this water will get thirsty again. But no one who drinks the water I give will ever be thirsty again. The water I give is like a flowing fountain that gives eternal life.'

JOHN 4:13

The holy well

There was once a gentle, beautiful girl who lived happily in a Welsh valley in Clwyd. She loved the hills and valleys of her home. She also loved Jesus. She'd heard all about him from her uncle, who was a very holy man. But one day a young princeling called Caradoc caught sight of her, and fell in love. She didn't want to have anything to do with him, but he persisted. He even pretended that he wanted to marry her. That didn't work, either.

Caradoc had a hot temper. His love for Winefride turned to hate. He vowed to be revenged for her rejection of him, and took out his sword. She ran for the safety of the church nearby but he overtook her, and swung his sword, intending to kill her. The story goes that her head was severed by Caradoc's sword, but that her uncle, calling on God, raised her from the dead. One thing is certain, and that is that she went on to live a long and happy life as a nun in her beloved Welsh valleys.

But at the place where she had fallen, a fountain of clear water sprang up. Soon tales began to circulate that this water was holy and had healing powers.

When Winefride eventually died in old age and her body was taken to Shrewsbury, many people went to pray to her there. Others continued to visit the Holy Well in search of healing. Two great English kings went there. King Henry V made a pilgrimage to the Holy Well on foot from Shrewsbury, as did Edward IV. The mother of another king, Henry VII, built a fine chapel to honour Winefride at the place we now know as Holywell.

The memory of the gentle girl lives on through the visits of the people who still visit her Holy Well and the chapel beside it.

Prayer

Dear Lord Jesus, let me learn about you more and more every day.

Suggested activities

A collage of the Holy Well

You will need:
- ❂ Paper
- ❂ Paints
- ❂ Pencils
- ❂ Scissors

Draw and colour figures of men, women and children from the 7th century onwards, and mount them on a picture as they visit the Holy Well. Include the two kings, and also people from today. Use the picture of the Holy Well building below as a guide for your drawing.

Well-dressing

You will need:
- ❂ A large (A3) piece of coloured card
- ❂ A felt-tipped pen
- ❂ Pictures of flowers cut from catalogues, or flowers made from tissue paper in different colours, crumpled and stuck in rosette shapes
- ❂ Scissors
- ❂ Glue or paper paste

Symbol

Mark out an oblong, square or circular shape on the card with the felt-tipped pen. Divide the shape up into a pattern of corresponding portions. Each portion is filled in with 'flowers' of a particular colour.

Well-dressing is a custom mostly to be found in Derbyshire, where real flowers are laid out to make a pattern before a holy well. Sometimes this is also done for flower festivals, creating a 'carpet' of flowers down an aisle of a church.

NB: Ellis Peters wrote the famous 'Brother Cadfael' books, with many references to the gentle saint Winefride both in Clwyd and in Shrewsbury.

Suggested songs

Be still and know (JP22; C19)
Deep and wide (JP35)

Reproduced with permission from *Stories of Everyday Saints* published by BRF 2002 (1 84101 224 6)

St Hilda

Key date: 17 November

7th-century friend and advisor of kings and bishops. Abbess of Whitby, educator, patron of Caedmon.

God blesses those people who make peace.

MATTHEW 5:9

The wise woman

Who do you think is the most famous woman in the world?

Until recently, it wasn't easy for women to have a career. Mostly they got married, had children and that was that. Hilda was related to the royal families of Northumbria and East Anglia, but although she was as good as she was clever, she didn't get married. Instead she went to serve God in a small monastery where everything was in a muddle. Once she'd sorted that out, she was sent to a much larger monastery at Whitby. This was a double monastery, which had one house for nuns and another for monks.

Hilda could have run a government department single-handed. She soon got things straight at Whitby, too. She made sensible rules for everyone to follow and saw that they were carried out. Common sense and kindness were her trademarks… and listening to what Jesus wanted her to do.

She encouraged everyone to study the Bible and take up good works. She even encouraged an illiterate cowman called Caedmon (whose story is also in this book) to compose his own songs. Soon the men who trained at Whitby were going out into the world to take up high positions in the Church. Everyone went to Hilda for advice, including kings and high officials of all kinds.

A tricky problem arose in the Church, which had everyone taking sides. Hilda was asked to act as hostess when everyone met to talk about it. At first Hilda urged one point of view, but when that was defeated, she made it her business to see that everyone went along with the majority view. If she hadn't been such a peacemaker, the two sides would have gone on fighting for ages.

She was such a loving person that she was called 'Mother' by everyone who knew her.

Prayer

Dear Father God, you have given us rules to follow in life. Please help us to keep them.

Suggested activities

Yes and no

Circle the things you should not do:

Be polite

Brush your teeth

Steal

Share your toys with a friend

Eat ice cream

Use swear words

Watch television

Hit people

Tell tales

Symbol

FOR OLDER CHILDREN

If you do wrong...

Talk about what happens to people who break the law. To live happily together, we have to respect one another and obey certain basic rules. Ask the children what they think these rules should be, and fill in any gaps in their knowledge. Touch on litter in the streets, graffiti, noise pollution, cigarettes, under-age drinking and, if appropriate, drugs.

Suggested songs

The wise may bring their learning (JP253)
Be still, for the presence of the Lord (K19; C20)

Reproduced with permission from *Stories of Everyday Saints* published by BRF 2002 (1 84101 224 6)

St Elizabeth of Hungary

'There was once a rich man who wore
expensive clothes and every day ate
the best food.'

Luke 16:19

The generous queen

A long time ago there lived a beautiful princess called Elizabeth. At 14, she was married to a man called Ludwig and went to live with him in his castle. Her new husband wasn't a bad man, but he thought only of pleasing himself. He didn't care that his people were suffering hardship, so long as he had beautiful clothes to wear, his castle was filled with beautiful things and there was a great feast in his hall every night. Every day he rode out hunting in the countryside.

It hurt Elizabeth to see that while everyone feasted at the castle, the poor people hadn't enough food to eat.

She asked Ludwig what he was going to do about the people who were starving in the villages nearby. He didn't want to think about such things, so he became angry with her and forbade her to interfere.

Knowing he wouldn't approve, Elizabeth slipped out of the castle every day with a basket of leftover food for the poor people. Of course Ludwig soon learned about this and lost his temper with her.

'Elizabeth, I forbid you to waste my money giving to the poor!'

But Elizabeth couldn't bear to think of the poor people going hungry when she had so much. So she went on doing it.

One hard winter's day, Ludwig caught Elizabeth going down to the village with another basket of bread.

'So, madam! I find you have disobeyed me! Show me what you have in your basket!'

Frightened, she asked God to save her from her husband's anger, and replied, 'It's only roses.'

Angrily he flung back the cover of the basket, only to find… a basketful of red roses! On a dark day in winter, the bread had turned to roses!

Prayer

Dear Lord, we can't feed everyone in the world who is starving, but remind us to give what we can to charities that can help.

Suggested activities

Bread... or roses!

Cut out and colour the shape of a basket filled with loaves of bread. Cut out and colour a bouquet of red roses. Cut a slot in the basket through which the bouquet of roses can be pushed up in front of the loaves of bread.

Symbol

A strip cartoon

Decide how many 'scenes', or pictures, you need for the story.

Only use one speech bubble for each character. If you have two speech bubbles in one scene, then the first to speak has the top left bubble, and the second speaker's bubble goes under and to the right.

Decide how each character can be drawn very simply. Elizabeth should wear a long dress with a cloak over it, and a light veil over her hair. Ludwig should have a short tunic with embroidery, belt, good boots and a big cloak over all. Poor people wear ragged tunics, with no shoes. The castle can be 'Disney' style. Villagers live in thatched one-roomed houses.

Reproduced with permission from *Stories of Everyday Saints* published by BRF 2002 (1 84101 224 6)

St Andrew

Andrew brought his brother to Jesus. And
when Jesus saw him, he said, 'Simon son of
John, you will be called Cephas.'

JOHN 1:42

'Don't be afraid! From now on you will
bring in people instead of fish.'

LUKE 5:10

The fisher of people

It's not always the people who talk loudest who make
things happen.

Andrew and his brother Simon were fishermen on
Lake Galilee. Andrew was the quiet one who thought a
lot about good and evil. He always wanted to hear the
latest preacher who talked about God. One day Jesus
was pointed out to Andrew. Straight away Andrew
realized that Jesus was the man they'd all been waiting
for. He went to tell his brother Simon that they'd found
the one man who really knew God.

Jesus went out on to the lake in Simon and Andrew's
boat and told them to let down their nets to fish—
although earlier they'd been fishing for hours and
caught nothing. Immediately, the nets were filled to
overflowing with fish. Everyone was amazed, but Jesus
said to them, 'Don't be afraid! From now on you will
bring in people instead of fish.'

Andrew and Peter left their boat and followed Jesus
wherever he went. Peter was the one with the loud voice
but Andrew was the one who quietly got on with the job.
When the crowds followed Jesus out on to the hillside to
listen to him speak, and there was nothing for them to
eat, it was Andrew who said to Jesus, 'There's a young boy
here with five barley loaves and two fishes.' With those
few loaves and fishes Jesus fed five thousand people.

The four people who lived closest to Jesus were
Simon Peter, John, his brother James—and Andrew. But
of these four close friends, it was usually Andrew whom
people went to when they needed to speak to Jesus.
Andrew was the one who always listened to what
people had to say.

After Jesus' death, Andrew travelled widely, especially
in Greece, spreading the good news wherever he went.
He became the patron saint of Scotland when some
mementoes of him were taken up to Fife, to a place
which is called St Andrews even today.

Prayer

Dear Lord, show me how to make a difference in the
world around me.

Suggested activities

Catch a fish

How many fish can you see swimming in the water? And whose fishing-line has caught the biggest fish?

Find the fish

Can you find the following fish in the wordsearch?

T	H	A	D	D	O	C	K
U	E	T	U	O	R	T	O
N	R	E	Q	X	Z	J	I
A	R	N	C	A	R	P	B
G	I	I	Y	N	W	U	T
N	N	D	C	O	D	Q	U
I	G	R	Z	M	X	P	B
T	B	A	Z	L	L	Z	I
I	J	S	H	A	R	K	L
H	K	Y	I	S	Z	Y	A
W	O	C	W	X	J	K	H
L	E	R	E	K	C	A	M

FOR OLDER CHILDREN

carp	haddock	herring	plaice
shark	tuna	koi	salmon
cod	halibut	mackerel	sardine
trout	whiting		

Symbol

Suggested songs

I will make you fishers of men (JP123)
Last day of November (BBP50)

St Nicholas of Myra

**Key date:
6 December**

4th-century
bishop. Legendary
giver of presents
to the deserving
poor. He also
raised three slain
children from the
dead. Patron
of children.

**The prayer of an innocent person is
powerful, and it can help a lot.**

JAMES 5:16

Santa Claus

Once upon a time there was a bishop who went around
doing good. Bishop Nicholas wasn't content to tell
everyone else how to behave. He put on ordinary clothes
and went out into the streets to see for himself what was
going on. And, if necessary, he did something about it.

For instance, he heard that one great lord had lost all
his money. This lord had three beautiful daughters, but
in those days, however beautiful you were, no one
wanted to marry you unless you had some money. The
girls were faced with starvation—or worse. Bishop
Nicholas knew that the girls deserved something better,
so he disguised himself as usual, went down into the
town and threw three bags of gold through the great
lord's window.

Now the three girls could marry and be happy.

Another day, Nicholas was travelling in the
countryside. There had been a famine and the poor
people hadn't enough to eat, but he came across an inn
where the landlord said he had plenty of pork.

This made Nicholas suspicious. How had the
landlord managed to obtain pork when no one else had
any? The story goes that Nicholas went into the cellar
and found a large barrel of salt water, and in it… shock,
horror! There were three small children, whom the
landlord had killed and was proposing to cook and eat!
Bishop Nicholas came to the rescue and raised the
children from the dead.

I wonder what happened to the evil landlord!

Even after he was dead, people still believed that
Bishop Nicholas could perform miracles. Once, when a
ship was sinking in a storm, the sailors called on him to
save them. He calmed the waves and saw them safely
to land.

Saint Nicholas is the patron saint of all children,
young girls and sailors.

Prayer

Dear Lord Jesus, help me to understand what I can do
to help other people.

 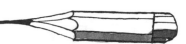

Suggested activities

Decorations on strings

You will need:
- ✿ Card
- ✿ Paint (preferably gold or silver)
- ✿ A paper punch
- ✿ Scissors and glue sticks
- ✿ Glitter
- ✿ Thread or wool
- ✿ Scraps of bright paper, ribbon or braid for decoration

Photocopy the templates for a star, a ball and a bag of money. These can be used to cut out the shapes from cardboard. Using a punch, make one hole in the top of each, and thread through some fine thread or wool to hang them up. Decorate the shapes with paint, glitter, ribbon or braid.

Symbol

Gifts without strings

Some people give presents only when they expect a gift back. Think about giving a present to someone who can't give you anything, who perhaps won't even say 'Thank you' for it. Think about those who won't get any presents at Christmas time, and see what you can do about it. Gifts of good toys, books or clothes can transform homeless children's Christmas!

Another way of making a gift at Christmas is to go carol singing (under supervision) and give the money collected to a children's charity.

Suggested song

You can be happy (God loves you) (K80)

Reproduced with permission from *Stories of Everyday Saints* published by BRF 2002 (1 84101 224 6)

St Thomas of Canterbury

**Key date:
29 December**

1118–1170.
Chancellor, later
Archbishop of
Canterbury,
quarrelled with
Henry II and was
slain by his
knights. Miracles
at tomb, which
became a place
of pilgrimage.

'You cannot serve both God and money.'

MATTHEW 6:24

The king's best friend

Has your best friend ever asked you to join in doing something wrong? And how did you react? It's not always easy to refuse, is it?

Thomas was a clever young man who saw that the way to fame and fortune was to ensure that King Henry II always had a good time. Thomas was a financial whizz-kid, so Henry made him Lord Chancellor. Thomas was brilliant with the king's money and a great success all round. But whatever other business he had to do for the king, Thomas was always there when the king wanted to enjoy himself.

It wasn't always easy being the king's best friend because Henry had a hot temper, but for some years everything went well.

Then Henry decided that he wanted Thomas to be Archbishop of Canterbury. Henry thought Thomas would be perfect for the job because he'd always done what the king wanted and would no doubt continue to do so.

Thomas didn't want to be a priest, but the king insisted.

Thomas thought long and hard. Could he still be the king's best friend and also serve God? He decided that he couldn't. He became Archbishop, but stopped doing what the king wanted and started working for God instead. Well, that did it! Henry was furious.

One quarrel after another led to the king uttering some wild words: 'How much longer do I have to put up with this?' Four of Henry's knights cut Thomas down in front of his own altar at Canterbury. Too late, the king was sorry for what he'd said. Soon the news spread that sick people had been cured after visiting Thomas' tomb. Even today people visit Canterbury to see the place where the king's best friend decided to be God's friend instead.

Prayer

Dear Lord Jesus, help me to say 'no' if I am ever tempted to do something wrong just because my best friend wants me to.

 **Suggested activities**

FOR YOUNGER CHILDREN

The make-over

Photocopy the picture of Thomas as the king's friend, and the clothes he wore as archbishop. Colour them in and cut them out. Then dress Thomas in his archbishop's robes.

FOR OLDER CHILDREN

The king's playtime

What do you think the king and Thomas enjoyed doing when they were in party mood? Circle the words describing what you think they did.

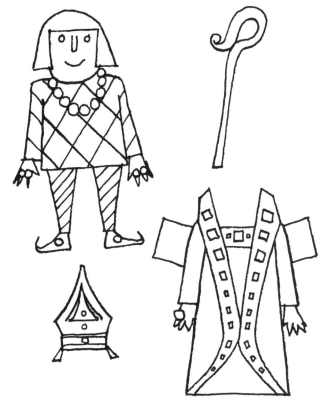

Eating	Flying kites
Playing loud music	Hunting
Playing cards	Fishing
Driving fast cars	Dancing
Watching TV	Riding
Playing computer games	

Sometimes, when we are having a good time, we become a little selfish and forget about the problems that we may be causing other people. Discuss what these problems might be—for example, dropping litter, playing music too loudly, spilling food and drink, rough behaviour.

Talk about enjoyments that might seem harmless at the time but have bad effects on our health later, such as smoking.

Symbol

Suggested song

Seek ye first the kingdom of God (JP215; C184; K292)

Appendix One

You will need:
- A large square cardboard box
- A4 size card
- Felt-tipped pens and paint
- Glue, Blu-Tack, paper straws
- An empty matchbox
- Dolly pegs or lengths of dowelling 8 cm in diameter, and pipecleaners
- Scraps of material, ribbon and wool
- Toy farmyard animals

1. Cut away two sides and the lid from the box. With a felt-tipped pen, draw tree silhouettes on the two sides, and a wide arc on the base. Cut to marked lines.

2. Fold 2cm down length of card. Glue this flap to represent the stable roof at left side at the back. Paint stable roof brown, and paint box sides green with a few tree trunks. Paint floor brown. Prop up stable roof with two straws painted brown, using Blu-tack to fix them into place.

3. Pierce back right wall near top for 'star'. (The children can take it in turns to shine a torch through.) Glue fine straw or hay wisps over stable roof and flooring. Use empty matchbox for crib, painted brown and stuck with the box on top of the cover. Cover with scrap of material.

4. For the figures of Mary and Joseph, shepherds and kings, use short (8cm) lengths of dowelling or dolly pegs. Faces can be made (eyes and mouth only) with a fine felt-tipped pen. Arms can be made by gluing pipe-cleaners round where shoulders should be. Cut tabards of material with slits for heads to go through. Cut head-cloths out of squares of fine material. Tie tabards round waists with wool. Glue and tie head-dresses in place with lengths of wool. Figures can be made to stand up with Blu-tack.

5. Baby Jesus can be made from a bundle of rolled-up pink silk. Animals can be borrowed or bought from a child's farmyard set.

DRAW TREE SHAPES, AND CUT OUT

FOLD

← CARD ROOF FOR STABLE

MATCH BOX MANGER

← STRAWS FOR SUPPORT

– BLU TAC TO HOLD IN PLACE

GLUE THE TWO TOGETHER

LINE WITH SOFT FABRIC

PAINT THE SCENE

JOSEPH AND MARY ARE MADE FROM DOLLY PEGS

ARMS ARE PIPE CLEANERS

YOU CAN INVENT CLOTHING FROM SCRAPS AND RIBBONS

THE BABY JESUS IS MADE FROM PINK SILK WRAPPED IN COTTON AND TIED WITH RIBBON

Appendix Two

Be a good reporter: create your own newspaper

This activity can be used with any of the stories in this book.

> **You will need:**
> - Two sheets of A3 paper, folded in half
> - Pens
> - Rulers

The newspaper can either be produced on a computer or it can be written in *black* biro on ordinary paper, using a lined sheet beneath it to act as a guide.

Decide on a title, for example, *The Thames Times*. Appoint an editor, whose decision is final. Appoint people to work on different specialities, such as writing news stories, sports reports, poems, environmental studies; making up jokes; creating illustrations, banner headlines; doing illustrations, and so on.

There should be an illustration or a photograph on every page.

Suggestions for content

Front page and page 2: Reports on school visits to a museum, or individual trips, such as to Disneyland. Other news items, such as an end-of-term play or concert, or a visit of specialist teachers from outside. Include a short poem at the bottom of page 2.

Page 3: The short story should be illustrated and *must* fit into one page.

Page 4: The fashion page should be illustrated. Leave room for a short poem.

Page 5: An advice or agony column might address bullying or some other problem, and might include a health report or report on the school's or an individual's animal(s).

Page 6: Reviews should all be short. Editor needs to be strong here!

Page 7: Jokes can be as corny as you like. Adverts/swaps on lower part of page.

Page 8: Sports page—try for reports on several sports, not just football.

The pages are put together by cutting out articles, pasting them into place, writing in bold headlines, and photocopying them. Provide one copy for each member of the group. The layout might look like this:

Page 8	1
Sports page	Title and front page
	News with photos and pics

2	7
News items	Jokes, adverts and swaps
Short poem	

4	5
Fashion	Agony aunt
Short poem	Environmental study

6	3
Reviews	Short story

Alphabetical index of the saints

Bible reference: Jesus said, 'Put your finger here and look at my hands!' (John 20:27)

St Frideswide (c.680–727) **74**
Key date: 19 October

The princess who fled the powerful king of Mercia through the forest. He was temporarily blinded but recovered due to her prayers.

Bible reference: Be kind and tender-hearted to one another, and forgive one another, as God has forgiven you through Christ. (Ephesians 4:32, GNB)

Bob Geldof, KMG **56**
(Knight of the Order of St Michael and St George)
Key date: 13 July

The pop singer who in 1985 roused the world to action against starvation in Africa by setting up Band Aid and Live Aid.

Bible reference: To everyone who is thirsty, he gives something to drink; to everyone who is hungry, he gives good things to eat. (Psalm 107:9)

St George (4th century)....................................**34**
Key date: 23 April

Patron saint of England and of soldiers. The legendary slayer of the dragon, who rescued the princess.

Bible reference: We are not fighting against humans. We are fighting against… rulers of darkness… So put on all the armour that God gives. (Ephesians 6:12–13)

St Hilda (7th century)....................................**80**
Key date: 17 November

Friend and advisor of kings and bishops. Abbess of Whitby, educator, patron of St Caedmon.

Bible reference: God blesses those people who make peace. (Matthew 5:9)

St Hildegard of Bingen (1098–1179)....................................**66**
Key date: 17 September

Musician, artist, naturalist, visionary. Influential Benedictine abbess in Germany.

Bible reference: I will praise you, Lord! You always do right. I will sing about you, the Lord Most High. (Psalm 7:17)

St John the Apostle (died late 1st century) **42**
Key date: 6 May

Jesus' much-loved disciple, writer of the Gospel of John. Patron of writers.

Bible reference: God loved the people of this world so much that he gave his only Son, so that everyone who has faith in him will have eternal life and never really die. (John 3:16)

St Joseph (1st century) **40**
Key date: 1 May

Foster-father of Christ, husband of the Blessed Virgin Mary, patron of fathers of families and manual workers, especially carpenters.

Bible reference: Joseph was a good man. (Matthew 1:19)

St Joseph of Arimathea (1st century) **26**
Key date: 17 March

He took Jesus' body and put it in his own tomb. His staff became the Holy Thorn of Glastonbury.

Bible reference: Joseph went to Pilate and asked for Jesus' body. (Luke 23:52)

St Kentigern (Mungo) (died 612)....................................**8**
Key date: 13 January

Bishop of Strathclyde. Originator of the legend that gives Glasgow its arms of ring and fish.

Bible reference: When you give a feast, invite the poor, the crippled, the lame, and the blind. (Luke 14:13)

St Luke (1st century)....................................**72**
Key date: 18 October

The Greek doctor who kept Paul on the road. Author of the Acts of the Apostles and the Gospel that bears his name. Patron saint of doctors and artists.

Bible reference: Our dear doctor Luke sends you his greetings. (Colossians 4:14)

Martin Luther (1483–1546)....................................**14**
Key date: 18 February

Leader of Reformation, inspiration for rise of Protestantism.

Bible reference: You cannot make God accept you because of something you do. God accepts sinners only because they have faith in him. (Romans 4:5)

Martin Luther King (1929–1968)....................................**30**
Key date: 4 April (also third Monday in January, USA)

Leader of the US black freedom movement. Nobel Peace Prize winner.

Bible reference: On us who live in the dark shadow of death this light will shine to guide us into a life of peace. (Luke 1:79)

St Mark (died c.74)....................................**36**
Key date: 25 April

Author of the Gospel that bears his name. Cousin of Barnabas, companion of Paul and Peter. Patron of Venice.

Bible references: Mark, who is like a son to me, sends his greetings too. (1 Peter 5:13)

This is the good news about Jesus Christ, the Son of God. (Mark 1:1)

St Michael....................................**68**
Key date: 29 September

Archangel, and commander-in-chief of the forces of good against evil. Guardian angel of the Hebrew nation.

Bible reference: A war broke out in heaven. Michael and his angels were fighting against the dragon and its angels. But the dragon lost the battle. It and its angels were forced out of their places in heaven and were thrown down to the earth. (Revelation 12:7–9)

George Muller (1805–1898) **22**
Key date: 10 March

Founder of Bristol orphanages. He supported missions, orphanages and schools worldwide by 'praying in' gifts.

Bible reference: When you welcome even a child because of me, you welcome me. (Mark 9:37)

John Newton (1725–1807)....................................**58**
Key date: 24 July

Once a slave trader, on his conversion he worked to abolish slavery. Later he became a clergyman and wrote the hymn 'Amazing Grace'.

Bible reference: But God treats us much better than we deserve, and because of Christ Jesus, he freely accepts us and sets us free from our sins. (Romans 3:24)

St Nicholas of Myra (4th century) **86**

Key date: 6 December

Bishop, and legendary giver of presents. He raised three slain children from the dead. Patron of children.

Bible reference: The prayer of an innocent person is powerful, and it can help a lot. (James 5:16)

Florence Nightingale (1820–1910) **44**

Key date: 12 May

Founder of trained nursing as a profession for women.

Bible reference: The Spirit has given… the power to heal the sick. (1 Corinthians 12:9)

St Patrick (5th century) **24**

Key date: 17 March

A slave in Ireland for six years. Returning to England, he was made a bishop and sent back to Ireland, where he fought paganism and banished snakes.

Bible reference: I trust you to save me, Lord God, and I won't be afraid. (Isaiah 12:2)

St Paul (died c.65) **54**

Key date: 29 June

The great apostle who first persecuted Christians, and then took the good news to the Gentiles.

Bible reference: Christ… sent me to tell the good news. (1 Corinthians 1:17)

St Peter (died c.64) **52**

Key date: 29 June

Jesus' right-hand man and leader of the Christian Church after Jesus' death.

Bible reference: Jesus asked… 'Simon son of John, do you love me?' Peter answered, 'Yes, Lord, you know I love you!' 'Then take care of my sheep.' (John 21:16)

Albert Schweitzer (1875–1965) **10**

Key date: 14 January

Nobel Prize winner, musician, philosopher, doctor. Founded and worked in a hospital in French Equatorial Africa.

Bible reference: 'I am the way, the truth, and the life!' (John 14:6)

Lord Shaftesbury (1801–1885) **38**

Key date: 28 April

Although nobly born, he fought for the poor—especially the chimney-sweep children.

Bible reference: God is Spirit, and those who worship God must be led by the Spirit to worship him according to the truth. (John 4:24)

Mother Teresa (1910–1997) **62**

Key date: 27 August

The little nun who founded the Missionaries of Charity, begun in India but eventually reaching worldwide. Nobel Peace Prize winner.

Bible reference: When I was hungry, you gave me something to eat, and when I was thirsty, you gave me something to drink. When I was a stranger, you welcomed me, and when I was naked, you gave me clothes to wear. (Matthew 25:35– 36)

St Thomas of Canterbury (1118–1170) **88**

Key date: 29 December

Chancellor, later Archbishop of Canterbury, quarrelled with Henry II and was slain by his knights. Miracles at his tomb made it a place of pilgrimage.

Bible reference: You cannot serve both God and money. (Matthew 6:24)

St Winefride (7th century) **78**

Key date: 3 November

Virgin, beheaded as she fled from a neighbouring prince, but restored to life. A fountain with healing powers sprang up on the site.

Bible reference: Jesus answered, 'Everyone who drinks this water will get thirsty again. But no one who drinks the water I give will ever be thirsty again. The water I give is like a flowing fountain that gives eternal life.' (John 4:13)

Reference and song books

Oxford Dictionary of Saints, Oxford University Press, 1997

Hall's Dictionary of Subjects and Symbols in Art, John Murray, 1986

Bede, *History of the English*, Penguin, 1960

Encyclopaedia Britannica

Servants, Misfits, and Martyrs by James C. Howell, Upper Room, 2000

Herbs and How to Know Them by Mary Thorne Quelch, Faber & Faber Ltd, 1946

Who, Me? Paul by Veronica Heley, BRF, 1998

Is That It? by Bob Geldof with Paul Vallely, Penguin, l986

George Muller by Roger Steer, Harold Shaw Publishers, 1985

The Big Blue Planet, Stainer & Bell (shown in the text as BBP)

The Children's Hymn Book, Kevin Mayhew (shown in the text as C)

Junior Praise, Marshall Pickering (shown in the text as JP)

Kidsource, Kevin Mayhew (shown in the text as K)

Sound Bytes, Stainer & Bell (shown in the text as S)

Story Song, Stainer & Bell and the Methodist Church Division of Education and Youth (shown in the text as St S)

'Do They Know It's Christmas?' is included in *Christmas Singalong*, Music Sales, and is also available as a single sheet (IMP Code 9783).

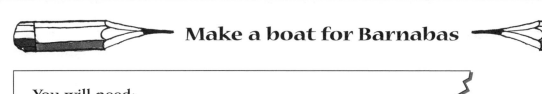

Make a boat for Barnabas

You will need:
- ✿ Crayons or paints
- ✿ Cardboard and coloured paper
- ✿ Drinking-straws and glue

Make a paper boat, following the diagrams below and instructions overleaf.

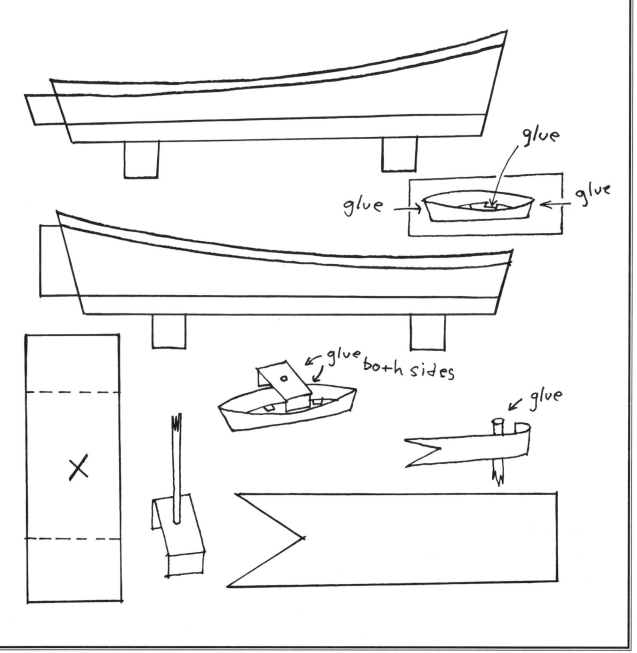

 **Boat instructions**

1. Photocopy page 95, carefully cut out the two sides of the boat, the 'bridge' and the flag, and colour them in.

2. Paste the sides of the boat and the 'bridge' to some flexible card. Glue each end of the boat together, and at the same time glue the tabs to a piece of cardboard large enough to support the boat.

3. Make a small hole in the 'bridge' (where the little cross is) with the point of a compass. Don't make it too big, as this is where you will have to put the mast (made from a drinking-straw).

4. Now bend the 'bridge along the dotted lines and glue it into place across the width of the boat, with the tabs inside the boat.

5. Glue your straw into the bridge and tie another straw diagonally across it. You may need to put a spot of glue on the end of the diagonal straw to hold it in place on the bow of the boat (see below).

6. Carefully cut a triangle of paper and glue it along the length of the diagonal straw.

7. Finally, curl the flag around the top of the mast and glue it into place.